Advance Praise for *The Devil Never Sleeps*

"Juliette Kayyem is who we call when disaster strikes for a reason: she's calm, unafraid, and deeply informed. Here she leaves no disaster unturned as she shows how we can be ready to respond. She'll open your eyes: you'll definitely never think of Fukushima, fires, or even Beyoncé the same way again."

—Erin Burnett, CNN anchor, *Erin Burnett OutFront*

"From 9/11 through the pandemic, the United States has been battered by several decades of emergencies. Even more, and worse, are ahead. Juliette Kayyem has a clear-eyed, sane, urgent-but-not-frantic set of principles to guide us in dealing with 'the devil.' We'll all be better off for following her advice."

—James Fallows, National Book Award winner

"Juliette Kayyem's infectious energy and passion for reasoned crisis management jump out of the pages of her book. She has written a succinct, compelling kitchen-table tutorial on how to get your head around crises—which are increasingly the normal state of affairs. As she makes clear in her down-to-earth, practical style, we don't have to panic, react, and wring our hands when disaster descends upon us, as it inevitably will. A must-read for first responders, crisis managers, and the normal citizen who wants to anticipate, prepare, cope, and be resilient."

—James Clapper, former national intelligence director

"Juliette Kayyem combines real-world national security experience, the everyday personal experiences of a private citizen, and the genius of a policy thinker for her compelling and engaging new book, *The Devil Never Sleeps*. Virtually anything Kayyem writes is a must-read, and she has put it all together to help us prepare for our era of disasters."

—Jeh Johnson, former secretary of homeland security

"We live in a dangerous world where big trouble is inevitable. Oddly, those who warn us to be better prepared are often dismissed. But Juliette Kayyem refuses to be a modern-day Cassandra. Get your head around this book and get smart. Or ignore her lessons at your own peril."

—Miles O'Brien, correspondent, *PBS NewsHour*

"An eye-opening look at the disasters that have troubled humans throughout history—and why they seem to be increasing in frequency. . . . An urgent, useful survival manual for our time."

—*Kirkus*

THE DEVIL NEVER SLEEPS

THE DEVIL NEVER SLEEPS

LEARNING TO LIVE IN AN AGE OF DISASTERS

JULIETTE KAYYEM

PublicAffairs

New York

PublicAffairs
Hachette Book Group
1290 Avenue of the Americas, New York, NY 10104
www.publicaffairsbooks.com
@Public_Affairs

Printed in the United States of America

First Edition: March 2022

Published by PublicAffairs, an imprint of Perseus Books, LLC, a subsidiary of
Hachette Book Group, Inc. The PublicAffairs name and logo is a trademark of the
Hachette Book Group.

The Hachette Speakers Bureau provides a wide range of authors for speaking events.
To find out more, go to www.hachettespeakersbureau.com or call (866) 376-6591.

The publisher is not responsible for websites (or their content) that are not owned by
the publisher.

Library of Congress Control Number: 2021953008

ISBNs: 9781541700093 (hardcover), 9781541700109 (ebook)

LSC-C

Printing 1, 2022

To my mom and dad
and
to all those who help when others need it the most.

CONTENTS

THE DEVIL NEVER SLEEPS

PROLOGUE

The boys were restless. We all were. It was April 2020, and we had been home, isolated, sheltering for just over a month. They were learning, if it could be called that, remotely after their high school shut down a few weeks before. Their older sister had returned from college, displeased that her freshman year would end taking classes from her bedroom at home. We were all stuck in our house in Cambridge, Massachusetts. Although I, as their mother, might occasionally admit it was special to hold them captive again, they found no such benefits in the situation. As far as the pandemic went, though, we were lucky. Our complaints derived from inconvenience, not wrenching sorrow.

Built in 1840, our rambling and cranky house took a bit of a beating with three teenagers back inside all day, every day. We had spent years tugging it into the modern era, but its bones were still old. It held up well enough for its age—until a fan broke.

In the boys' second-floor bathroom, the ceiling covers what we had believed was a small crawl space. Above, on the third floor, is my daughter's bedroom and a guest bedroom, with storage closets built in nooks and crevices around a slanted ceiling. Behind the closets, an architect had told us, were small crawl spaces that we could ignore, as they had been closed off for so long. So we had lived for a decade not really knowing what was behind those third-floor back walls that hid the space above the second-floor bathroom ceiling.

In April, the boys' bathroom ceiling fan stopped working. They didn't tell me. They said they forgot. Instead, as kids will do, they continued to take long, hot showers, oblivious to what the lack of ventilation was doing to the plaster. I would later wonder, Did they not notice the paint chipping? The ceiling plaster eventually fell in a big clump, exposing the crawl space above on the third floor. But it was much more than that. A long, narrow space, only about four feet high, was discovered. Our masked handyman set a ladder and hauled himself up. There was nothing in there; no animals or furniture, no treasure. We found just a single mottled photo.

The photo captured a distinguished-looking man leaning on a railing, a red-tinted drape and chair behind him. There were a few words on the back, a name, a date. I was fascinated and very curious. Who was this man? I took the mystery to Twitter, where I knew online genealogists lurked. Surely someone would know what to do with this. Twitter delivered by the hundreds. There was a lot of speculation about the print, the card stock, and the tinting. In about an hour, Twitter sleuths found out where I lived (it's that easy?) through property searches and worked backward from newspaper stories and historical documents. The photo was of a relative of the McCue family, who had lived in my home, their home, from 1917 to 1919.[1]

I should probably admit here that my immediate obsession with this search was also a consequence of the pandemic's manipulation of our time, of the concept of time. I, too, was home, distracted, not really myself, though busier than I had ever been. I no longer traveled; an airport fixture, I would not get on a plane for eighteen months. Still, I was not idle in 2020. My career in disaster and crisis management, preparing public and private entities for what they least expected, was in demand. Whether in academia, government, media, or the private sector, I like to say I have had many jobs but one career. I am like a storm chaser—but for disasters in general. I have a reputation for remaining calm when others do not, and my mantra has

Photo of a McCue family member, found in the author's home.

always been to "pace the rage." I have low blood pressure, literally and figuratively.

This profession has led me to places around the globe, many of which have recently experienced a wrenching, often seemingly unfathomable catastrophe. One such place was the small town of Joplin in Missouri. That is where the title of this book first came into view. There I met with Jane Cage, a widow. When a tornado killed more than one hundred of her neighbors and friends as it raged up Nineteenth Avenue in the midsize God-fearing town in 2011, she found herself at a crossroads. I met Jane when I visited Joplin a year later, the sort of anniversary event that we do to memorialize those we lost and celebrate how far we have come. The event was emotionally strange, unsure of itself: Was it a party or a funeral? Was it gross or nice that the lead "hurricane hunter" from the Weather Channel was there signing autographs?

I met a mother worried that high school classes were still in trailers and anxious for the new facility to be ready. I talked with a father who spoke of house renovations without mentioning why he had so many rebuilding projects. There was a couple who had just moved to Joplin, recruits for the hospital, who were curious: they did not know what the town had been like before. Jane Cage did. And she hadn't loved everything about the place she called home. The traffic was heavy and squeezed out pedestrians and bikers, there was racial segregation across train tracks, and the town had few public spaces. Joplin was not a perfect place. When the tornado struck, too many people died because systems weren't working, alert warnings were delayed, and the community was not informed of what to do fast enough. For that year and the years after, Jane Cage led an effort to make Joplin better and ready for the next disaster.

Her determination was infectious. Maybe it was her faith, a belief in something bigger. But I came to think that was a simplistic, maybe even condescending explanation. Hers was a faith grounded in something quite tactical, operational, realistic. She wasn't praying for deliverance or that Joplin would be spared when she knew that it would not be. There would be more tornadoes. She had no delusions but was still optimistic. She told me her guiding principle:

"The devil never sleeps. But he only wins if we don't do better next time."[2]

In the years since then, I have come to believe it. Surely, we all know this now. Disasters and crises are not one-offs, random events, rare occurrences; they are standard operating procedure. I say this to be liberating, not dispiriting. Disasters are simply no longer random and rare. And once we can all accept this lived reality—that the devil never sleeps—then we can better prepare for when the next one comes because it will come, as will all the ones after that. So much of our discourse about disasters focuses on the past and why we didn't prevent them or on the future and how to stop them from happening again. But we live in an age of disasters. They are here, and they are not going away. There will be tragedies, but they will be tragedies made less tragic if we commit to sustained preparedness to minimize their consequences. And so I taught and wrote and traveled the world in the hopes that we might also see opportunities from events we never asked for.

And then, in 2020, everything stopped. And I was home in the rambling, cranky house whose history was about to be discovered when the bathroom ceiling fell.

We did know something about our house, but not about the McCues. Previous owners in the 1920s had served dinners here and advertised with local publications: "REAL HOME-COOKED FOOD: Daintily Prepared, Properly Cooked and Served, try Elizabeth's Home Dining Room." A blowup of this advertisement is now a framed poster in my kitchen, an inside joke with a family that tends not to eat "daintily."[3] The McCues were the owners immediately before Elizabeth's meals were served.

The Twitter hunt continued for hours, complete strangers sending me information through the platform about the mystery of my walls. Charles McCue, a salesman, had been very involved with the local high school, then called Rindge High School, and served on the school committee. Rindge is now Cambridge Rindge and Latin School, one of the oldest public high schools in the US. My kids were enrolled there, coincidentally. Annie McCue was born Annie Davies, and her parents lived down the street. Annie and Charles had two children. A son, born in 1900, died in 1902 from spinal meningitis. They also had a daughter. Charles died in 1935, his obituary describing him as a "valiant spirit."[4]

It seemed like a great find, but before I went to bed that night, I learned that Charles and Annie's daughter, Elizabeth Letitia, also attended Rindge High School. Known only as "Jack" to her father, Letitia was his frequent companion to Elks Lodge meetings and on

'IA McCUE

Barne's Pri-

Elizabeth Letitia McCue, given to the author from Sarah Leslee on Twitter.

sales trips west. Letitia, it seemed, was her father's life. A Twitter friend found a picture of her in the school newspaper.

I fell asleep thinking of this turn in events in which a basic water leak led to this early twentieth-century family. The following morning, I woke up to something sad, even disturbing. The Twitter genealogists had discovered more. Letitia died in our home in the early days of January 1919 at the age of nineteen. Her small funeral was also held here, as the newspapers reported, with influential political and academic leaders sending their prayers. Massachusetts governor Calvin Coolidge, who would later become president, "was one of the first to send his sympathy."[5] The family moved out soon after.

Then I was sent her death certificate.[6] Letitia died in the third of four waves during the Great Influenza epidemic, often known by a misnomer, the Spanish flu. That pandemic lasted from February 1918 to April 1920 and would infect about a third of the world's population at the time—about five hundred million people—before it ended. The death toll is uncertain, but estimates put it between twenty and fifty million. Letitia's death certificate describes her cause of death: "Influenza." One hundred and one years later, as we waited out another pandemic, we were living where she had died from the last one.

At that time, homes were built with infirmary rooms that, ironically, were often used for both bringing in life during a home birth and easing toward death for the sick or old. They were isolated from the main area for privacy and to protect the healthy. In my home, that space was on the third floor, eventually hidden behind the back wall of a closet. Letitia entered it when she caught the flu. She never left it alive. When she died, they built the wall. A picture was left behind.

Annie, Letitia's mother, died a widow in Cambridge in 1962. She had lost a son to a childhood illness and a daughter to the last great pandemic. Later during that week of discovery, a family member of the McCues, who had been forwarded the Twitter thread, contacted me. She told me more about the family. I immediately mailed the picture of the distinguished man, likely Annie's father, that we found in the crawl space. It was hers.

I was distracted and amazed by all of it. If you believe in karma, you might find it here. I wasn't quite sure how to react. There was the irony of a modern family, stuck at home during this pandemic, finding a picture of another family who suffered during the last one. Or the coincidence of my work as a disaster and homeland security expert, so much of it being about the 2020 pandemic, ricocheting back to the walls that confined and protected us at home. Or the reminder of the known progression of pandemics—Letitia's death, a warning that misery comes in several waves. Or the shared worry of two mothers from different eras trying to protect their nineteen-year-old daughters from a deadly virus.

Maybe the lesson is simpler, obvious. I live in a rambling and cranky old house that has seen much since it was built in 1840. Our home. The McCues' home. Two pandemics unite us across a century because the devil eventually returned.

INTRODUCTION

WHAT'S IN A NAME?

A disaster is often defined as a sudden, destructive event that brings with it great damage and loss. Its original meaning, from Middle French and Old Italian, comes from the Latin prefix *dis*, signifying a negative force, and *astro* for star. Stars were blamed because of the belief that their alignment influenced the fate and future of humans.[1] It was thought that when something bad happened on earth, it was a reflection of some ill-fated star pattern. With this definition, disaster is too often viewed through the lens of luck; the word *catastrophe* also shares the *astro* explanation. These meanings put humankind in a passive position, at the mercy of forces we cannot control, always surprised by what the constellations may bring.

This description of a disaster may be antiquated, but it still has hold. In the course of writing this book about crisis and disaster management, I came to believe that the word itself had set us on a course of amnesia, excusing our shock and awe, as if we had no agency to manage these disruptive occurrences. After the horror, we just want to move on, bury the dead, pick up the debris, and heal our wounds. It is a very human instinct—to move on from the past and to assume that because we have survived, we have coped. We buy bumper stickers or hold memorial concerts named for the city that has been destroyed—New York, Boston, Paris—adding the word *strong* to signify our supposed resilience. Emotions, not tactics, guide our sense of success.

As I write this, the world is still roiled by the COVID-19 pandemic, with its recurrent waves and seemingly endless variations. Fresh from this experience, surely, we all know the proverbial stars will misalign again? The Texas ice storm that eviscerated the state's electrical grid? A large tanker ship stuck in the Suez Canal? A hack against our gas pipelines? Perhaps a hurricane? A flood? A wildfire? A drought? A Miami apartment falling to the ground? A Travis Scott concert? Space debris? The list is endless. Where even to start? Where to end?

This spoil of riches is the point. For there to be a start, it assumes a finish. For the war to end, it assumes there was once peace. For you to stop worrying, it assumes there was a time of unicorns and rainbows when days were carefree and weightless.

I'm here to disabuse you of that notion. There is no finish line.

So much of our discourse about responding to disasters has ignored the potential to do better now. We focus on the past and future, but not on the present. We debate how best to prevent climate change that causes flooding. We seek long-term resiliency in response to that flooding. As for our capacity to succeed on the day of the flood, well, that's up to the stars.

There will be a devil next time, and the next time, and the next time, and the time after that. Its lessons are for all of us because we must all consider ourselves disaster managers: the CEO and government leader, the teacher and student, the small business owner and the middle manager, the mom and dad. None of us, we all know now, is immune from a devil whose tricks range widely: climate catastrophe, cyberattack, terrorism, pandemic, or a mass shooting. We look one way, fearful of a threat, and from behind comes the next. The devil is indifferent to any of our desires to give it just one name, to delegate it to some other person's responsibility. So we must better prepare through an era when our connectivity is both a strength and a vulnerability. We must accept this fact, the stars are misaligned, and position ourselves with the tools and skills to be better prepared to respond to the events as they come.

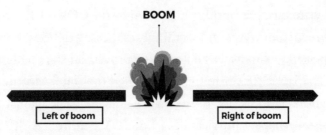

The two sides of a disaster framework.

And in that positioning, we can respond to these recurring disruptions in ways that make us more likely to minimize the harm, though harm will still surely come.

To do so, this introduction describes the basic contours of disaster management and where they have failed us in the past. Disaster chasers tend to divide the world into two moments: left and right of boom, before and after the disaster. It isn't this simple; there are subdivisions and pieces to each side. But the binary division is conceptually accurate. Essentially, when we think of a disaster, we focus on all the things we can do to stop it from happening (left of boom) and then all the things we can do to pick up the pieces when it does (right of boom). Subsequently, we view success as keeping to the left of boom and failure as right of boom.

It is a consistent framework for those of us in the field. Imagine looking at a timeline of a generic disaster. The left-of-boom stages describe the investments and policies an institution, a business, a government, or an individual makes to avoid it from happening. These are the prevention and protection efforts to delay or dodge the devil. They can be big projects, such as a missile defense system or a nation's carbon reduction plan, along with the simple ones we per-form day to day, such as putting a light on a bike at night or clearing out storm drains to deter water backup to protect our home. We don't think of these ordinary things as left-of-boom investments, but that is exactly what they are. We are trying to avoid the disaster or at least minimize the consequences should it arrive.

Yet despite best efforts, the "boom" will arrive. The boom may be a crack, a rumble, a surge, an electric fizzle, a howl, a deadly quiet. They are all booms: disaster management is about being ready for any boom in any shape, for whatever the devil brings. This concept, known as *all-hazards* planning, does not focus on one specific hazard but instead on all of them. Some specialized threats may need specialized reactions—a fire is, in fact, different from a cyberattack—but fewer specialized reactions than we may think. Accepting both the commonality and frequency of disasters allows us to focus on the few key skills needed to manage them rather than highly specialized measures that belong to limited environments. Booms can be slow or fast, wet or dry, hot or cold, silent or loud, visible or invisible. It does not, it should not, matter. It will come. So we must focus on the right-of-boom activities, which are all those things we do to respond, recover, and build more resilience once the devil has arrived, again.

This book focuses on those commonalities and about how we can live more confidently in anticipation of the right of boom, nurturing our immediate responses again and again and again. I want to make disaster management simple, accessible, because I no longer believe that it can be a unique skill delegated to professionals. Disasters, whose impacts know no limits, must be prepared for by disaster managers, which, ultimately, is every one of us. There are basic features and skills that are called upon that need not be secret. These efforts are not solely for a specific type of harm or a single disaster. They apply universally, perpetually. We know them now. By highlighting the recurring features of disaster management, we can, as a society, overcome some of the fallacies and limitations that have affected the field for too long.

Mostly, we need to stop being surprised. If we can structure ourselves around the probability, not the mere possibility, that we will sometime, somehow, always be on the right side of the boom, then we will better invest and nurture the capabilities and skills that can minimize the harm that is to follow. We will get over the notion of what is often experienced as the *preparedness paradox*, the outcome of being successfully prepared for that one single disaster, resulting in the disaster either being avoided or its impact lessened. Naysayers will then believe that the investment was unnecessary because the consequences were less than anticipated. Instead, sustainable twenty-first-century disaster management doesn't take place during a single moment in time or focus on a single event. It recognizes the widest ongoing and recurrent potential for disaster: it treats the devil seriously, knowing that the devil never sleeps.

My goal is not to dwell too much on the pandemic in these pages. I use the pandemic to expose how, despite its viral novelty, it followed the same disaster framework that guides all others. Since all of us have lived through it, it will be easy, if not maddening, to see how it unfolded according to a known cadence. To the left of boom were all the efforts to better protect food supplies, detect a global pandemic, inform, educate, and even prepare for its inevitable arrival by buying masks or surging supplies. Not enough of that happened, of course, and many nations spent the early part of 2020 squandering that time, looking at the efforts in China and then Italy from a distance, hoping the boom wouldn't come.[2] It did. And the response and staggered recovery, from flattening the curve to staying at home to masking and eventually a vaccine, were ways we collectively and individually adapted once we were to the right of the boom. The pandemic was scary, but it followed an oddly familiar framework, like a predictable surprise.

The devil will come, but to assume that we are ready because we accept this fact is giving ourselves too much credit. Screaming that the sky is falling isn't exactly going to save lives, protect property, and prepare communities and our families better. The nature of recurring disasters, and positioning society for them, is to admit that preparations for them are never complete. We would be in grave danger if we assumed some finish line; the nature of the devil is that you never quite catch up to him.

And that means that we need to look at success differently. True, stopping a climate disaster or a cyberattack is a measure of success;

putting locks on your home door is an important investment to stop an intruder. What any of us wouldn't give to live, always, on the left side of the boom. But we can't; we won't. We need a different metric. We must now view success through the lens of what I call *consequence minimization*. Simply, did we do enough so that our entry to the right of the boom will result in less horror, not none? We can make things *less bad* by sustained preparedness. Accepting that we live on the right side of the boom, we can judge our investments best by whether our individual and institutional planning and preparedness means that fewer people died or less was damaged. The measure of success here is not that we can avoid the devil, only that his constant return will be less tragic.

Working in this field, I wish every day that those who spend their time trying to eliminate risk succeed. I have three children whose lives will soon be built far from mine; I would welcome a world that remained on the left side of the boom. As a society, government, and individuals, we need to do everything we can to stop the bad from coming: mitigate climate change, minimize radicalization, protect cyber networks, identify public health dangers immediately, alert populations to impending doom. I'm all for it. But this is not a book about climate mitigation or how to counter radicalization. I take those, and other harms, as a given.

But to accept defeat shouldn't leave us helpless. Success need not be binary, where either the disaster happened or it didn't. There is no role in our lives that is immune to catastrophe. The following chapters provide the steps necessary to brace for the recurring disruptions. The objective is to stop us from being in a situation where we are wringing our hands and asking only, "How did this happen this time?" and instead help us see the recurring themes, successes, and failures that will better prepare us for the inevitable times ahead. Based on fieldwork, the work of experts and practitioners, reports and commissions, history, some imagination of what might have been, and the reflections of people who have been in the scrum (coincidentally, all interviews were done on Zoom due to the pandemic), the legacy of past disasters will be assessed—sometimes counterintuitively—and explored for the lessons for today.

Each chapter examines crises from the distant and near past to draw eight important common lessons that can be implemented now to prepare us for our inevitable future of recurring disasters. Chapters 1–3 focus on the essential building blocks to prepare for the boom: an acceptance that prevention will fail, established mechanisms to listen and communicate as the disaster unfolds, and structures to enforce unity of effort to respond to the crisis. Chapters 4–6 highlight best practices to limit the harms unfolding on the left side of the boom: avoiding the last line of defense crutch, constantly testing response systems, and training how to "stop the bleed." Finally, chapters 7 and 8 lay out tactics to pivot and learn in time for the next disaster.

These steps are not mutually exclusive. Take one, two, a few, not in order. They are an effort to crystallize the management and leadership skills for all, in whatever roles, that worked or failed in disasters of the past after the boom came. The benefit, if it can be called that, of an era of catastrophes is that there is no dearth of material. A review of them as a group rather than each individually illuminates consistent guideposts for how to position ourselves better time and time again. These lessons focus us on a single moment, that minute before the impending boom, and what we might have wished we had done. It turns out "woulda, coulda, shoulda" is actually a pretty good standard for preparing for the devil.

The book ends with a call to action. We need to reject the fantasy of a fictional place we have deluded ourselves into believing in, a place where we can claim some sort of victory. It doesn't exist. Instead, we must think in terms of a place that positions us more safely as we wait for the devil's inevitable return. We are here, now, and that is success.

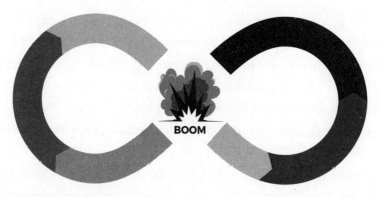

Reoccurring disaster framework.

If we think this ends, then the devil wins. We can always do better next time in this infinite loop of destruction.

THERE ARE NO SURPRISES

Disasters are the standard now. They are not the aberration, but the norm. We surely must know that as we shift from one tragedy or surprise to another. Yet I feel that the fact we can't seem to get our heads around the potential for disaster and prepare for it in rational ways is a testament to the power of positive thinking. We just live our lives, go about our days; maybe there are a few random emergencies and blips, but consistent disruption seems beyond our thinking.

It may not just be the power of positive thinking that leads to such willful blindness and short-term planning. Investments in the future are always more difficult as a policy matter, let alone a political one, than what is in the immediate box. Media headlines and Twitter noise capture our time and attention. To structure our institutions around constant and predictable disasters seems a paradox, after all. What is a crisis if it doesn't have an element of surprise?

In academic literature, there is a difference between a crisis, a disaster, and a catastrophe. A crisis can occur without any consequence; it generally means a threat to a fundamental system that absolutely, without question, requires a response. US Airways pilot Chesley "Sully" Sullenberger famously landed a distressed plane on the Hudson River when he ran out of time to get back to the airport, saving all passengers and crew in 2009. A potential disaster was averted because of his skills and composure, leading to the "Miracle on the Hudson."[3] A disaster comes when the crisis is not appropriately addressed and there is a horrific consequence. This is familiar territory for most of us; the raging California fires that can kill hundreds are the result of a small flame that burns out of control.[4] Finally, we then often call a poorly managed disaster a catastrophe. A catastrophe occurs when the crisis seems to result in more damage than it ought to have, such as the more than forty people who drowned on the East Coast after 2021's Hurricane Ida, which hit land in the Gulf Coast, continued to travel, and brought rain and flooding to people who believed they were safe in their basements.[5] For the purposes of this book, which focuses on how best to manage disasters and their consequences, the terms *crisis*, *disaster*, and even *catastrophe* are best understood as reflecting right-of-boom demands. They all describe a world after the devil has arrived.[6]

One of the most enduring explanations of the attributes of a crisis comes from Charles Hermann, a professor of foreign policy. He wrote that a crisis is an event with three distinct features: it "threatens a high-priority value of the organization," it "presents a restricted amount of time in which a response can be made," and it is "unexpected or unanticipated by the organization."[7] This is a mostly helpful definition, as it cuts to the core of what separates a crisis from a routine emergency or even a scandal. The exposure of an illicit affair or release of a sex tape of a corporate leader may feel like a catastrophe to the people impacted, but such a scandal most often doesn't threaten a high-priority value of the company. Hermann's definition focuses on what is actually at stake. It isn't just anything; it is *the* thing, its essence. The failure to deal with it means disaster ensues.

This definition, however, needs an update. There should be no more surprises. It is a question of when, not if. Of course, there are flukes and randomness, but even they present the same challenges to an institution that a more likely or an expected event would have. We believe in some unique thing called *crisis* because we still believe in surprises. As a result, we have a fascination with why we are not ready and less rigorous analysis on what it would take to be ready. For all of us, it can be made simpler: more left and right of boom, both, always.

True, to prepare for disruptions as a common phenomenon negates the very specialness of what makes a disaster, and that seems definitionally absurd. It isn't. It is like leaving an umbrella in your car in anticipation of rain. It isn't that it rains all the time, but that there is enough expectation of rain that it makes sense to be ready. We don't need to be surprised by the unexpected; we need to be ready for it. The focus on surprise as a precondition of a crisis definition has animated disaster management and planning. But it is not only obsolete; it is dangerous. It leads us to be paralyzed by a paradox.

THE PREPAREDNESS PARADOX

The paradox of preparation refers to how successful preventative measures can intuitively seem like a waste of time. It has such a stronghold on how we think about the potential for harm that it unwittingly tends to excuse the institution or person for failing to prepare. It makes us wary to get ready for fear that the very fact of getting ready will be paranoid, defeatist, or defensive even if the preparation is surely more likely to negate the impact of the disaster's consequences. This is known as the preparedness paradox. It keeps us from promoting preparation in anticipation of a bad event because the benefits of preparation are hard to see and therefore justify. After all, if we are prepared, then the harm won't be so bad, making others wonder why we were all so worked up in the first place. But the preparedness paradox is only a paradox because we have set up our evaluation of a disaster as an all-or-nothing experience: either it happens or it doesn't. That can no longer be the case. The more accurate assessment is whether the disaster would have been worse had we not anticipated that it would occur. In every case, the answer is yes.

Focusing our efforts on consequence minimization instead of just prevention means that all of us have the capacity to learn skills that reduce the harm as it comes at us again and again. Specifically, with large-scale, stretched-out events that have effects that are difficult to gauge immediately (COVID-19, climate change), it can be hard to spur people to action. The only way to get ahead of the curve, then, is to take actions at the time that may seem like overreactions. When the harm is limited or forestalled because of the preparedness, then people will think the effort of getting ready was unnecessary. It is like a school snow day that is called in anticipation of a storm that in the end never quite develops or skirts the city rather than dumping all over it. We roll our eyes, despair that our children are home unnecessarily, and urge the local leaders to be more robust next time. What we fail to account for is that even if the storm misses the city, it might have made some of the commuter routes used by teachers dangerous. Or if the snow falls as rain but then freezes, the dangers may be greater than from the snowfall. Or that the practice of closing down better prepared us for the next storm.

The prevention paradox was first formally described in 1981 by the epidemiologist Geoffrey Rose.[8] In that arena, it describes the seemingly

Preparedness Paradox

If they work, successful measures can often seem like a waste of time or investment.

contradictory situation where the majority of cases of a disease come from a population at low or moderate risk of getting sick, and only a minority of cases come from the high-risk population of the same disease. This is because the number of people at high risk of significant illness is normally small. So to prepare for the disease by focusing on the high-risk pool would often seem like a waste of time because it covered such a relatively limited number of people.

Before epidemiologists were household names, the preparedness paradox remained an obscure theory. It took center stage for most of us, however, nearly two decades later. To save memory space in computers during the onset of our digital lives in the 1970s and 1980s, the years were abbreviated—1999 became 99. When that year came, there was considerable concern that computers wouldn't know what year should follow 99: Was it 2000, 1900, or even 1000? The consequences of computers skipping backward a millennium was a major threat. If the computers became "confused," they could shut down, erasing bank and medical records, causing power outages, and freezing transportation systems.

This was the Y2K fear that animated much of technology preparedness in 1999. In late 1998, the US government passed the Year 2000 Information and Readiness Disclosure Act to encourage companies to get organized and prepared and to share methods of preventing computer meltdowns. The act also provided liability protection for companies so that they wouldn't be penalized for responding.[9]

Companies spent somewhere in the range of $300–$600 billion on preventing and preparing for Y2K. And when the clock struck at midnight on New Year's Eve, not much happened. Some thermostats failed in an apartment building in South Korea; a bus ticket device in Australia crashed; a few lottery machines in Delaware failed.[10] Given all the focus on the threat, the fact that nothing of major consequence occurred quickly created a different narrative: Why did people freak out so much? It is, for those in disaster management, a consistent and frustrating irony.

Safeguards prevent disasters all the time, but we seldom think or hear about them at all because "everything is fine" is not compelling news. Experts can wax eloquent about how various regulations were crucial to avoiding a catastrophe, but it is difficult to empathize much over something that didn't happen. It isn't just that we don't necessarily believe it, but that we also discount it in the future: It didn't happen this time, so why should it happen next? An action to prevent a disaster can be a self-defeating prophecy. Skeptics of the preparation will be able to say, "You all worry too much."

Y2K fears were, in fact, justified. These legacy computers were also the very systems that ran some of our most essential infrastructure, including air traffic control and banking. But when January 1, 2000, passed without so much as a minor catastrophe—though there was hoarding of food and water, the National Guard was on standby, financial markets were preparing to crash—a myth started almost immediately that the threat had been grossly, negligently exaggerated.

"The inherent conundrum of the Y2K debate is that those on both ends of the spectrum—from naysayers to doomsayers—can claim that the outcome proved their predictions correct."[11] The American public did not necessarily know how computers worked or how programming factored into the fears, and it therefore really had no strong equities in the debate about how much it should overreact. The prospect of a massive system failure seemed scary enough—and appealing enough from a media perspective—that it was accepted as fact. So when it didn't happen, skepticism became the norm. That all the retrofitting of mainframes might have saved modern society was quickly replaced by a different narrative. The fear and relief turned into derision, a bit of a punchline, because the warnings appeared unnecessary. It was seen as, wait for it, a "hoax."

But twenty-plus years later, that readiness had a very different narrative within the field. Y2K preparation worked; the threat was real. The clock, or boom, struck the year 2000, and little happened. The concerns made public awareness greater, even slightly paranoid, but it was the behind-the-scenes work in reaction to that fear that led to the preparations that made planners confident they could avoid catastrophe. The public doesn't remember it that way, though. Hence, the paradox. The only unavoidable response to the preparedness paradox then is a commitment to sustained preparedness; being ready will seem not that outside the norm.

THE WHY AND WHETHER

Essentially, I am sort of done with wondering why and whether and how likely bad things happen. Or, more specifically, I leave that to others, to those who study personality traits or probabilities. Tremendous scholarship and examination, for example, has gone into understanding why leaders do not prepare well for disasters. In their seminal book *The Ostrich Paradox*, authors Robert Meyer and Howard Kunreuther provide an accessible account of the six leadership biases that plague so much preparedness management.[12] They are pretty self-explanatory.

These attributes help explain why leadership so often fails us. They describe the internal motivations, or lack thereof, that make us unwilling

Six Leadership Biases

1. Myopia

2. Amnesia

3. Optimism

4. Inertia

5. Simplification

6. Herding

From *The Ostrich Paradox* by Robert Meyer and Howard Kunreuther.

to accept that the crisis will come. These are ways that we see no evil in order to convince ourselves that the devil does not exist. In the historic disasters that are discussed in the following chapters, these attributes can be seen and identified in the leadership of those who should have acted better. One must overcome these biases to be ready. Great! But then what? Once I've discovered my inner biases, what am I to do with that knowledge?

Much of risk theory has the same limitation in that it gets us to the right place—bad things will happen—but leaves us there. Much of risk analysis has now been influenced by the seminal 2007 book by Nassim Nicholas Taleb, a finance professor, an author, and a former Wall Street trader. Taleb's book, *The Black Swan: The Impact of the Highly Improbable*, was published a year before the 2008 financial disaster and became a global guide for industry and risk scholarship.[13] It was described by the *London Review of Books* as one of the most influential resources since World War II.[14] It changed the way many thought about predictability, and Taleb did so by basing the theory on a mere bird-watching event. For centuries, Europeans assumed that there were only white swans. That was true until black swans were seen in Western Australia by a Dutch explorer in 1697. That there were only white swans had been an "unassailable belief as it seemed completely confirmed by empirical evidence" until the black swans were discovered. In that moment, a universal expectation was invalidated.[15]

Black swan events—World War I, 9/11, the 2008 financial disaster—have three essential criteria. According to Taleb, the event is so rare that even the possibility that it might occur is unknown, it has a catastrophic impact when it does occur, and it is explained in hindsight as if it was actually predictable (in other words, it seems obvious after the fact). For such rare and extreme events, Taleb wrote, the standard rules of probability and prediction did not apply, and attempts to learn from statistics or models based on the past were actually much more likely to make us increasingly vulnerable to the black swan phenomenon. The past, in other words, was not a good guide for future risk. Taleb did not stop there, however, and his book is revolutionary for its additional contribution: since black swan events could not be predicted, it is essential that institutions—in particular, financial institutions—build "robustness" to negative events so that nothing can fail under the stressful conditions of the black swan event.

The impact of Taleb's book cannot be underestimated. The notion of the black swan came at a time after 9/11, the war in Iraq, and Hurricane Katrina, when the world was looking for an explanation of why bad things kept happening and why we seemed so unable to grasp them. But while examining the *whether* by utilizing a risk framework to determine a black swan—low-probability, high-consequence—event, Taleb leaves the nature of robustness for later. He'll get you to the right side of the boom, tell you that there are events that are consequential and unpredictable but not how to manage through the damage and destruction that will inevitably come.

Nearly a decade later, as both a compliment and a rejoinder, global analyst Michele Wucker wrote *The Gray Rhino*, examining our failures to recognize and then act on the obvious. The title refers to the

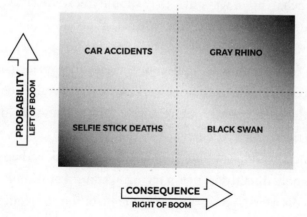

Risk calculation framework.

fact that rhinos are most often just gray. No point in looking for blue or pink rhinos, Wucker argues, but instead just look at what is in front of us, the risks we face every day and that are so obvious. The search for—and fear of—the black swan blinds us to the obvious threats in front of us. Repositioning the risk calculus, she argues for a focus on high-probability, high-consequence events that are always looming but never recognized.[16]

Taleb, Wucker, and others are essentially describing different quadrants of this chart, often used by risk assessors. Taleb's low-probability/ high-consequence event is in the lower right-hand quadrant; Wucker's high-probability/high-consequence event is the one in the upper right-hand quadrant. For the most part, risk assessment is just figuring out where the potential threat resides in the quadrant.

As the chart shows, risk generally can be measured, and investments focused, by considering the probability that a consequential event will occur and the harm that will occur if the event happens. As for the other quadrants, the risks that are both unlikely and with less impact can be written off: think of the couple of dozen people who die annually from Instagram-worthy selfie-stick photo behavior over the Grand Canyon or in front of the Taj Mahal. No matter how sad or careless, we shouldn't move an entire system of security to stop people from behaving in ways that they should know are risky. In other words, we sort of let Darwin take care of that pool. For the high-probability/low-consequence events such as fender benders, scraped knees, or some minor disruption of services that major companies experience hundreds of times a week, we can generally adapt easily because the consequences are relatively minimal and we are accustomed to the frequent occurrence.

Imagine a world, as we must now, where the risk is there, always. To put it more directly: let's stop trying to control probability when it comes to disasters and start trying to control the consequences. We spend so much time and energy on imagining we can predict with

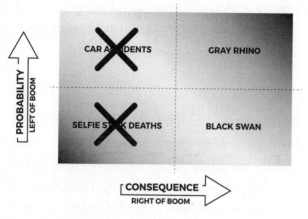

High-consequence risk calculation framework.

some precision what could happen when the more important realization is that it will. If that is the case, then the whole risk quadrant can be folded into a simple chart: low or high consequence. That's all you need to know. The words *unexpected, unanticipated,* and *unpredictable* will cease to be helpful guides or excuses: they are so passive and often in error.

In an era of recurring catastrophes, there are only two options: more or less consequential. We could change our entire way of thinking about disasters by accepting, instead, that they will come. I recognize that is asking a lot. Essentially, it calls for people to put aside momentarily the well-established field of risk assessment that calculates probability. In the end, though, the risk field prioritizes the actions on the left side of the boom. Instead, the lessons that follow make the case for measures of success on the right side of the boom based on the notion that whatever prevention and protections to the left of the boom have been undertaken have failed. Calculating what risks lie ahead has always been an art more than a science anyway. Entire intelligence agencies, insurance actuaries, and corporate risk managers work to put some quantifiable number to potential harms. Day to day, they often get it right: the earth is getting warmer, car accidents will always be more likely when the driver is a teen boy, or supply chains will be disrupted by weather events. But often they get it wrong. And the devil makes an appearance.

NOTHING IS THAT NEW

We all know it by now: the potential for disasters should be seen as the norm, not the aberration. Black swans and gray rhinos are everywhere. In left-of-boom prevention planning, the disaster management field has already come to this realization. Leaders talk in terms of all-hazards planning, meaning that the best security planning anticipates all types of potential threats. This reflects some of the lessons learned after 9/11. As money and resources were being distributed to state and local first responders to protect against terrorism, it became clear that the best investments were those that could be used to prevent any risk. After Hurricane Katrina in 2005, the industry shifted, as it realized that by focusing exclusively on stopping nineteen terrorists from getting on four airplanes, it meant it could not save an American city from drowning. Experts began to talk in terms of the notion of all-hazards, prioritizing those resources that protect against all sorts of threats and not just one. The devil could take any shape.

The same must become true for right-of-boom response. We need to talk in terms of same-consequence planning, akin to all-hazards prevention efforts. We already know the attributes of a disaster that we can train for. It isn't rocket science. Disasters are bigger, more disruptive, interconnected, forcing increased pressure on those who respond and increased scrutiny and activism by those watching. Those are the elements of the disaster that are known now. We can build for the common attributes and challenges of all disasters because, in the end, there is nothing special about them. They just keep coming.

Disaster management studies is moving in this direction, trying to find the connective tissue across every major disaster regardless of what preceded it. As Professors Arn Howitt and Dutch Leonard have documented, we can begin to see their similarities rather than any unique features.[17] First, disasters require that we recognize novelty and effectively improvise a response to that novelty. Second, they will inevitably demand some massive scaling; they are big and cross all sorts of physical and professional boundaries. Third, one of the greatest challenges will be maintaining what is called *situational awareness*, a greater emphasis on determining what is going on and therefore what is needed, which can be hard in the middle of the response itself. Fourth, the crisis response will succeed not just because the problems were planned for but because the response can pivot in real time; too late is always the wrong answer in a crisis. And finally, a true disaster will be bigger than what was planned for, with all sorts of people and interests coming forward and raising new concerns. It will be messy.

The disasters and their consequences highlighted in this book, spanning time and geography, embrace these commonalities. In a world where the devil never sleeps, where Y2K could happen every day, any planning measures will seem like prudent actions, smart preparation for the inevitable. Investments and preparedness won't seem like overkill because the danger will come. The preparedness paradox goes away because every day that there isn't a disruption isn't seen as a normal day but an abnormal one.

It may seem I am asking for overreaction, 24-7. But that is only a criticism if one sees overreaction as a bad response. Underreacting—maybe because the opposite seems hysterical or a waste of time or overwhelming—can, indeed, make something that might otherwise be just an emergency turn into a calamity. In 2014, a major snowstorm hit Atlanta.[18] Or rather, it was major for Atlanta, even though it was only a few inches in the end. But as the storm came barreling toward a city very unacquainted with snow—it had few snowplows—roads came to a standstill and students and employees were stuck. You may wonder, "Well, how can Atlanta possibly have been able to prepare for that?" Atlanta, however, certainly has weather forecasts, reads the paper, has friends in other cities, and has contacts with emergency planners up north. It did not position itself for what might happen. The city failed to use familiar blizzard response protocols, which are quite simple: everyone stays home. Unfortunately, once the authorities finally realized this should be the instruction, they then foolishly released everyone simultaneously, making the icy roads crowded, stranding people in some instances for eighteen hours.

No surprises. The devil may have plenty of time, but he has no new tricks. On January 4, 2020, I read a short article in the newsletter *STAT*, a partner publication of the *Boston Globe* focused solely on science and health news. It was a piece written by reporter Helen Branswell, who would become a must-read throughout the pandemic. It was headlined, "Experts Search for Answers in Limited Information About Mystery Pneumonia Outbreak in China."[19]

It seemed strange at the time, enough to pique my interest. The report spoke of a unique virus in Wuhan, China, one that was sufficiently worrisome that the Chinese were calling in the World Health Organization, even though they kept insisting they had it under control and that there were no deaths. That seemed odd to me, even though I'm no epidemiologist. China would have been unlikely to raise any concerns, let alone call in an international organization, if this was just an ordinary virus.

So I started to pay attention. The US government seemed reluctant to acknowledge or prepare for what was going to happen; through January, it was clear that overreacting was not going to be our problem. Then alarms started to sound. Wuhan was quarantined. Italy was brought to its knees. But in the US, we couldn't quite convince ourselves that this distant problem would soon, inevitably, be ours too.

Along with many others, I began to raise my voice about what was likely to happen. I prepared the kids, my home. I told friends to get ready, answered texts, urged my parents to hunker down in California. I started to get criticism about my public worrying. "Shut it down," I told Anderson Cooper on CNN, where I am a national security analyst, one night in early March during an NYC pandemic town hall he was hosting with Dr. Sanjay Gupta.

Cooper replied somewhat incredulously, "When you say shut it down, do you mean—" to which I interrupted, "Everything."[20] My mother texted to tell me she thought I sounded harsh. I was scaring people. That was my point. The devil was on his way. But we weren't ready, and any preventive action when there were so few cases of COVID-19 in the US seemed borderline paranoid.

"You are getting me nervous," Dante Ramos, an old friend and senior editor at the *Atlantic*, wrote to me. He had been noticing my Twitter feed, which had become a bit of a megaphone, and sensed a rare panic in my tone. He asked if I would write for them. The *Atlantic* would stand out throughout that first pandemic year for providing some of the best coverage and analysis.

So I wrote what I was worried about: the devil was coming. "What will you call it?" I asked after filing the essay.

On March 8, 2020, my piece "The U.S. Isn't Ready for What's About to Happen" appeared and found a big audience, probably because it validated a growing sense of public unease.[21] It warned of what soon was going to happen to the American public. "Especially at this point, even a more vigorous response will not preclude a lot of people from getting sick. Preventing all infections is no longer a possibility, and the measure of success is how much public-health authorities can reduce the number of people who die or fall seriously ill," I wrote. Reading it now, I realize that I was already on to consequence minimization; the risk could not be eliminated. Dante later told me he initially worried the title was a bit alarmist. As it turned out, within a few weeks, the piece proved relatively accurate. Strangers wrote to me to thank me for the advice at a time when the national leadership offered little. People knew that something didn't seem right, that a dangerous event was on the horizon, but felt that they were alone.

I wasn't prescient. None of us sounding the alarm in early 2020 were clairvoyants. We just knew the science. There was a virus. It was not contained. People moving around the globe would spread it. It should be no shock; indeed, it would be inevitable that it would hit us. However much we pretended or wished otherwise, it was coming for us. The devil was on his way.

The measure of success would surely be, for a pandemic, whether we had prepared enough—overreacted, even—so that the consequences would be less burdensome. This is a hard standard to accept. We tend to assess situations in a binary way, whether a thing is good or bad, black or white. But in a world of disasters, the ultimate judgment is always in the gray zone. A pandemic that kills fifty thousand people is surely better than one that kills six hundred thousand.

As COVID-19 came into focus in mid-March, Professor Ian Bogost also wrote in the *Atlantic* about the need to overreact to the impending doom.[22] He felt alone in his personal preparation as he watched family and friends continue with their day-to-day lives. What was it about overreacting that made people not want to prepare, resulting— as we soon saw—in a much greater challenge as the pandemic spread? To overreact is essentially to "look a fool" and be willing to go forward anyway. Long ago, Bogost noted, overreaction was actually viewed as something one could not control, like a muscle instinct. There was no moral judgment to it; blaming someone for overreacting was like blaming them for blinking during a sandstorm.[23]

That changed in the 1960s, and Bogost attempted to point to what might have caused this change toward a moral judgment, even condemnation, of preparation. One reason may be the rise of psychology and psychiatry as a profession and the resulting compulsion to explain every emotion and response. Overreaction was no longer seen as something objective, without moral judgment, but a state that was more akin to a neurosis. To be a neurotic, after all, is hardly a compliment and is understood as a failure to control one's emotions. It is, in the end, like being a little crazy. The second phenomenon that led to the denigration of overreaction was *financialization*. In the post–World War II economy, speculation was on the rise as the fundamentals changed. Supply-chain management, for example, often responded wildly to extreme perceptions of financial changes that were not tied to the reality of the market and were harmful to businesses.

Whether due to changes in psychology or the global market, or both, overreacting became worthy of moral condemnation and judged a waste of resources. It was viewed as an individual failing and an institutional defect that had to be overcome rather than nurtured. It became a "sin." "We went wrong when we allowed overreaction to become synonymous with reaction run amok: a crazed, irrational type of action rather than a legitimate way to respond, given a fundamental inability to understand and process stimuli effectively," Bogost wrote.[24] The bar should surely be higher for complaints of overreacting since disasters are now common.

True, judging an event based on how few people died or how much damage was reduced isn't particularly heartwarming. In the case of the pandemic, response planning also seemed loose and ever-changing: don't wear a mask, wear a mask—could someone please make up their mind? To be ready at that moment, those seconds, before the devil's boom will require constant behavior change. It may just seem easier to accept a level of harm, worry, complain, freak out, but still get on with our lives with no action. We could. But it hasn't been a great strategy so far.

We must flip our criteria for success. After each disaster or catastrophe, we are too familiar with taking up an old two-word refrain as our rallying cry: "Never again." Guess what . . . it will happen again. We must move dramatically, faster, and more realistically from a posture that is purely focused on threats to one that can make us better able to manage the consequences when we can no longer hold off the damage. We need to talk less about fears and more about needs. Are we safe? No. Can we be safer? Most certainly. We must brace for the boom.

"Never again" misleads us into believing in a finite and permanent version of success. In a world where one thinks of disasters as random and rare, that might be a perfectly realistic ambition. If occasional disasters were made ever-more infrequent, perhaps, eventually, they would cease to bother us altogether. But what if they are not occasional, not random, not rare? What if the devil never sleeps?

Every disaster has a history. Disasters hold our attention because of the harm we see, but also because they hold a mirror to what we are and the society and institutions we have built. Disasters find victims as they are, not as we want them to be. They expose all that is already wrong in a society: an earthquake in Haiti becomes a time to reflect on America's military and political excursions into the nation that have left it impoverished; a hurricane in New Orleans becomes a time to manage the racial and economic inequalities that emerged over hundreds of years from a city that used to be the center of the slave trade; a nuclear meltdown in Fukushima, Japan, becomes a time to critique the forced amnesia that overcame a country ready to move on from the nuclear attacks during World War II by neglecting oversight of a dangerous industry; an oil spill in the Gulf of Mexico becomes a time to debate our dependence on offshore drilling and whether we should move more swiftly to greener energy sources; a pandemic sweeping across a great nation, bringing it to its knees, becomes a time when we can no longer ignore the inadequacies and inequalities of its public health system.

We see the horrors brought by the crisis itself, but also the horrors already there. A disaster ends, but in the process, it reveals our identity, culture, and the systemic problems we have too long ignored. We might have been able to live in our blissful ignorance indefinitely but for the devil arriving in a flurry of wind, water, or fire, exposing our systemic negligence. If, when that disaster ends, we move on because we believe the disruption was an aberration or a surprise, we will not examine the deprivations and inequities that lead to such horrible consequences in the first place. The devil will have won the round, and he will return all the sooner.

THE NEW GOAL LINE: CONSEQUENCE MINIMIZATION

For the left-of-boom world, we try to minimize possible harms in our lives every day through what is known as *layered defenses*. As the phrase implies, these are the impediments or barriers that can slow the likelihood of a threat. You arrive at an airport. Your ticket and the information you shared have already been assessed to ensure you are not on any no-fly lists, that your information is valid, that you are allowed to travel. Your drive to the curb is monitored by surveillance and patrol cops. You go through the frustrations of the TSA line. The gate is another checkpoint. Perhaps there is a US Marshal on the flight. And, of course, there's a lock on the cockpit door. Layers upon layers upon layers minimize any risks associated with flying, crushing it down as close to zero as possible while still allowing millions to fly every week. We have no similar terminology for the right side of the boom, of how we should view success when all seems chaotic and lost and disastrous. This is the planning gap that must be filled because so much damage can be avoided and so many deaths eliminated.

It is, I admit, a variation of the notion of so-called acceptable losses—a chilling moral concept. One dead is better than ten. Ten dead is better than one hundred. One hundred dead is better than one thousand. The military accepts, indeed plans, around the notion of acceptable losses, comparing the mission's benefit with the likelihood of mass casualties. For the most part, it doesn't pretend that it can keep the number at zero. At times, the calculated cost in lives is seen as acceptable if the mission is necessary.

Knowing that the disaster will arrive means that preparation isn't for some distant future, relegated to the "later" box. You are here.

Right now. The disaster looms, and there are only a few minutes until it comes. The chapters ahead provide lessons about how we might better our readiness for that moment. We can live better, more successfully, on the right side of the boom that is bound to come. This will mean that a new strategy, a new metric for success, is needed. What if we no longer viewed success according to whether a disastrous thing occurred (left of boom) but instead according to what the consequences of the occurrence were (right of boom)?

So this is where we are. Here, as the boom arrives. We've all been in that moment when we find ourselves in a complicated, unfamiliar territory and rely on the big map with the bright, orienting marker: YOU ARE HERE. That in-the-present starting point is precisely what's been missing in the debates around disasters. We talk about prevention and what to do to stop bad things from happening. We urge resilience and how to recover stronger or, in today's parlance, "build back better" in the aftermath of a disaster. We focus on *before* or *after*. We talk too little about *here*: the moment, the situation before us, and what we can do to make this tragic moment a little less tragic. This book represents an effort to change that thinking.

I will constantly return to the refrain "You are here." It is meant to place us in the moment, right now, as we wait—years, months, weeks, days, maybe just hours—for the devil to arrive. It is meant to be grounding, to put the immediacy of preparation at the forefront. Reality is somewhere between total neuroses and extreme vulnerability, between the black swan and the gray rhino, in a space that accepts that disasters will come. Given the commonalities across all disasters, we know now what will prepare us better when the boom does happen, again and again. No surprises. There's no way back. Each chapter focuses on ways to minimize the consequences, because ten is better than one hundred dead. This isn't rocket science, but it is a science of sorts. Ten dead is, in fact, scientifically better than one hundred dead. *Less bad* is our standard of success.

We can't wait anymore because the harms keep coming, each new one unprecedented and therefore beyond our previously lived experience. We may not be able to stop them sooner than we can minimize their consequences. In September 2021, a handful of low-income people drowned in flash floods in basement apartments in New York City. They were not the first people to die in New York. They were not the first to be living in inadequate, not-fit-for-purpose spaces. They were, however, the first to drown. New York's historic poverty had collided with climate change that brought as much rain in two hours as the city usually sees in a month. The storm overwhelmed stairwells, underpasses, and subways. And because the most intense rain came after dark, it trapped some people who were sleeping.[25]

There is no way to reverse the harm done. Instead, we must focus forward to the next moment when the boom happens so that we will be better prepared. The eight steps ahead connect disasters over the centuries, gathering lessons that prepare us for the unremarkable fact that we surely know by now: harm will come when the devil returns, but he only wins if we don't do better next time.

There will be a next time. You are here.

CHAPTER ONE

ASSUME THE BOOM

"Mayday" Is a Day Too Late

In 2018 and 2019, two separate Boeing 737 MAX aircraft flown by Lion Air of Indonesia and Ethiopian Airlines, respectively, plummeted from the skies, killing a total of 346 people. The crashes were, it turned out, the result of a design flaw in a new feature—known as the Maneuvering Characteristics Augmentation System (MCAS)—that could overwhelm the pilots at times, limiting their capacity to control the plane. Boeing knew this and had a plan: the pilots would override the system should it falter. The problem was that in the event that untrained pilots were unable to override the MCAS that controlled the airplane nose, the plane would go down.

The story of the Boeing 737 crashes is like watching a horror movie where you see the killer under the bed as the victim rests her head on the pillow. You want to yell, "Don't do it! Look at what could happen," but no one is listening. Indeed, there were cautionary whistleblowers at Boeing, those who understood the magnitude of the MCAS design flaw and also understood that relying on pilot training required more than what Boeing was doing. Curtis Ewbank, a Boeing engineer, was one. He tried to warn company executives that the MCAS was unsuitable and cautioned against putting the airplane in the air. He was ignored.[1] Boeing had a single plan: the MAX had to fly.

Boeing's push to get the MAX into the air was purely about winning the market. When its competitor, Airbus, released its own version of a similar plane, Boeing rolled out the 737 MAX before it was ready. That would take a significant sleight of hand. Boeing would have to present the plane as new for sales, but not so new that it would be required to undergo the rigorous Federal Aviation Administration (FAA) regulatory process mandatory for new aircraft. Boeing was therefore presenting to the purchasing airlines that the MAX was spiffy and unique while arguing to regulators that it wasn't so spiffy and unique that they had to delay putting it in the air. Boeing did this by basing the MAX on an old design so that many of its safety features dated from the old 737 design and were not updated to new FAA standards. And to reduce costs to the airlines, Boeing insisted that no extensive training was required to fly the old-but-new MAX. The newness of the MCAS feature was minimized and not even briefed to pilots at first. The MAX was just a better version of the 737—think Botox rather than a facelift—Boeing told the world.[2]

If the Lion Air flight was tragic and unforgivable knowing the systemic problems with the MCAS, the later Ethiopian crash was devilish. Boeing had time to do something in the interim. Instead, it treated the Lion Air crash as a one-off. There was, as there always is, some evidence of a fluke; certainly, we can reduce any tragedy to the particulars of that moment. For example, the Lion Air aircraft, Flight 610, had just been sent to maintenance because of faulty triggers in the angle-of-attack (AOA) sensor vane that triggers the MCAS. When that aircraft was sent to be fixed, the AOA sensor was replaced with a secondhand, allegedly recalibrated AOA. That replacement wasn't done by Boeing or overseen by the FAA. The single replacement, which triggered a system that pilots had no knowledge on how to overcome, was done by Xtra Aerospace, a repair facility in Florida. The problem was that this new sensor was, tragically, miscalibrated. The fix was broken, so to speak.[3]

You can't find much about Xtra online except that it is closed, and a statement on their website insists that they did nothing wrong. But any complicated system that is exclusively dependent on a small company not screwing up a calibration of a device that is intended to protect the plane is a system that is doomed for failure at some point. On the first flight after calibration, the plane experienced serious problems with a forced nosedive because of the faulty AOA signal. The pilots may not have responded adequately, failing to follow a checklist that had been provided for just these circumstances. They tried twenty-six times to overcome the nosedive until the plane literally flew into the Java Sea. One hundred eighty-nine people were on board. All died.

"The final investigation report into the Lion Air crash states that this sensor was miscalibrated so that the angle it registered was 21 degrees too high."[4] A day after that report was released, the FAA shut down Xtra, revoking its aviation repair station certificate. Boeing took refuge in the idea that a freak combination of circumstances explained the crash: what were the chances that an AOA signal would be so disastrously calibrated; perhaps pilots from a country like Indonesia were not as sophisticated as American ones (this racism would pervade the later crash analysis as well); and so on. So between the AOA and the non-Western pilots, Boeing convinced themselves that they were not responsible for the circumstances of the Indonesia crash. Boeing immediately issued guidance to pilots about how to overcome the potential for nosedives in this new-but-not-so-new plane. It did not, remarkably, mention the MCAS specifically, again. Worse, in that same period between the crashes, the FAA would determine that the plane's MCAS was faulty and, without immediate action, would be at "high risk" of more accidents, up to one crash every three years.[5]

Well before three years, indeed just four months later, Ethiopian Airlines Flight 302 went down in March 2019. As far as we know, the AOA vane was sheared off by a bird strike, and the pilots couldn't

compensate for the MCAS activation. One hundred fifty-seven people on board died. The crew, according to the cockpit's black box
audio, had tried to follow Boeing's new guidance, but it is unclear
whether they did so correctly. After the second disaster, the 737 MAX
jets were finally grounded for nearly two years.

TO THE LEFT, TO THE LEFT

Any planner, leader, or manager has to embrace the potential for
disaster as a given. Planes will falter; vanes will be miscalibrated;
pilots will be undertrained or overwhelmed. These aren't excuses;
they are givens. Structuring our safety on the myth that these will not
be true is hopeless. Acknowledging this fact isn't defeatism, but
instead should motivate us to rethink where we place the boom. One
does not need to be an aviation expert to know that once the plane is
falling to earth might be a little late.

Like many disasters, however, the Boeing MAX crisis is often studied for all the wrong reasons. First, many make it out to be about an
evil company hell-bent on profits. This isn't totally inaccurate, but it
misses the more important point: companies are often hell-bent on
profits, after all, but not all invite disaster as a result. Second, many
assess how Boeing communicated after the tragedies. That is, essentially, inconsequential. Did Boeing spin this well? Could they have
spun it better? No amount of spinning—once the MAXs failed—
could help Boeing. "No talking points can save New Orleans from
Hurricane Katrina" is a common phrase in crisis management to
remind teams that an effective response is the only, and best, PR plan.
It's a helpful reminder not only for communications teams, but also
for studying disaster management.[6]

A different take would focus on consequence minimization, and
not on a greedy CEO or a careless postaccident communications
strategy that caused more harm than it needed to. Airplanes are

inherently complicated. We accept risk in complex systems. They will have challenges, defects, systems, including the human components, that do not always perform optimally. What that means is that the structural engineer who designs such systems must accept both the high and low probability of a harm coming to pass and minimize the consequences should that happen. And here is the forgotten news: Boeing knew. This is key; the company understood there was a risk involved in the redesigned plane. Boeing believed it was mitigating that risk by saying it would focus on pilot training. Fair enough—if true, it was a good plan. Any complex system should have redundancies, actions, or equipment that can compensate for a failure.

Shift the lens. Step to the left a little. We tend to think that the planes going down is the disaster, but that is a little too late. It is the MCAS failure that is the boom. Once the pilots lose control of the airplane, there are no other options but catastrophic impact. No institution should ever get to that moment when the consequences of failure are all or nothing. Boeing had an inherently unstable device; that isn't unique. But knowing that, its failure to provide alternatives, known and trainable, to that instability is inexcusable. It recognized a vulnerability, but it didn't let others know. The others, mainly pilots, were then surprised when the vulnerability inevitably exposed itself.

Boeing didn't nurture the tactics that would avoid catastrophic losses. If it had, then pilots would have been better prepared, training would have been mandated, and AOA sensors would have been treated with greater care. Most pilots didn't know about the MCAS and didn't know how to manage any failure. The Lion Air pilots did not even know of the existence of the MCAS or of their capacity to override it. Pilots around the world were not formally notified until two weeks after the Lion Air jet had crashed and were told to just cut the electrical power to the tail should they experience a malfunction. Boeing was hiding the tools to avoid catastrophic loss.

With technology like that of an airplane, the consequence minimization practices have to occur well before the pilot loses control and the plane plummets from the sky. There are many moments of potential doom in the making of the MAX, but that is going to be true of any complicated engineering system. What plagued the airplanes was that Boeing never took consequence minimization seriously. If the MCAS failed, Boeing knew that there was only one way to limit the consequences of that failure, which was to train the pilots. It was an easy fix, it was cheap, and it would have been consequential.

The MAX was a new plane sold as an old plane, and so the new features were not adequately trained for because to do so would mean that the plane was considered new, which would delay its rush to market. What the hell was Boeing thinking? Some of it came down to a culture that had over time deemphasized safety as a primary focus. For years, it was well known in the industry that the vast majority of aviation fatalities came from the simple act of a pilot losing control of an aircraft in-flight. At the same time, the FAA—the only US airline safety agency—had become less aggressive, more passive, in asserting its regulatory authority over the industry. Boeing, defending its market position against its primary rival, was fearful the market was moving forward without it.

It could be said that the MAX crisis began as early as 1997.[7] That was when Boeing merged with one of its competitors, McDonnell Douglas. That merger combined two leaders in global aviation and created a behemoth. At the time, it was the tenth-largest merger in US history.Boeing kept the name, and McDonnell Douglas kept the corporate feel.[8] Boeing was once the gem of American aviation, much like NASA was seen as a pristine, incorruptible agency with the smartest folks in the room. A culture shift toward financial management trumping everything else began to express itself after the merger, a shift that included the alienation of employees who had once viewed themselves as part of a family.

Indeed, the notion of the Boeing "family" was part of its connective tissue until the new leadership explicitly described the workforce as a "team, not a family," Dominic Gates, a *Seattle Times* reporter who won a Pulitzer for his coverage of the MAX disaster, told me. Gates has described the culture shift, which introduced outsourcing and a focus on penny-pinching, as the significant factor at Boeing that led to the 737 MAX disasters. "Think about what that shift means," he told me. "A family can't expel anyone. You learn to work together, work over differences. A team is a new tone. It means you have to carry your weight, and that is defined by corporate. But before, its employees had an emotional connection to the company. They had pride in making planes."[9]

This analysis isn't meant to minimize the responsibility of individuals in leadership, only to highlight that their failures are often more complicated than that they were bad, careless people. The caricature of an evil CEO, with his or her enabling deputies, carelessly making business decisions based solely on money and greed, impervious to the implications for employees, society, and safety—a Gordon Gekko from the movie *Wall Street*—is unhelpful because it is so simplistic. Greed does animate many of these companies, but the reasons why disasters happen are much more complicated: leadership, corporate culture, technology, money, luck, and so on. We must assume that no leader actually wants to enter the other side of the boom because the boom is disruptive to business continuity. It would seem obvious, then, that the primary motivation ought to be to ensure that the mechanisms that could force him or her there—a faulty system, a carelessly built structure, a weak cyber network—must also be built to minimize the consequences of any disaster.

Was Boeing leadership factoring in risk, consciously arriving at its own definition of what I described earlier as the equivalent of "acceptable losses"? Dominic Gates doesn't think so. "Boeing's entire business was that its customers understood that the product is safe. Its engineers and employees travel on airplanes, they understood that. Nobody could rationally make such a calculation, a deliberate risk. Instead, it really was an issue of groupthink, one that is part of corporate culture."[10]

It wasn't that Boeing was calculating some acceptable loss. It wasn't thinking of the loss at all.

GET YOUR HEAD AROUND IT

I don't mean to denigrate my work or say that those of us in it aren't sophisticated or knowledgeable, but it is safe to say disaster preparedness isn't rocket science. We don't make vaccines, create low-emission cars, or, for that matter, make rockets. What we do is messy, chaotic, consequential, but not intellectually hard. It is all really quite manageable as long as we accept one foundational principle: don't fight the boom.

To practice for disaster management, we often run simulations and exercises, what we sometimes call tabletops, to describe sitting around a table with the right people to practice policies and test systems. I am often amazed, or maybe dumbfounded, at how the initial reaction by a leader to some simulated emergency is to explain why, in fact, that crisis could never occur. No way, they tell me, this simulation is poorly constructed or too fictionalized. Instead, they prefer to focus on something familiar that they have already recognized as a stress test, mostly because they often know exactly what to do. They don't want to be surprised. They don't believe they will be surprised. They are denying the boom.

The lesson, time and again, is that the boom is coming. "Get your head around it" is my simple five-word refrain to wake the hell up. In a real-world scenario, nobody is going to have much patience for your explanation that what is happening couldn't possibly be happening. It is happening. Get your head around it.

Boeing's unwillingness to adequately define its moment of boom is not, in any way, an aberration in disaster management studies. In late 2014, Sony was set to release a totally awful but completely mesmerizing (I have watched it multiple times for my research, so this is a compliment) movie called *The Interview*. It was a comedy based around a plot to assassinate North Korean leader Kim Jong-un. The pivotal scene is surreal. Actors Seth Rogan and James Franco, after a long hunt for the elusive North Korean leader, finally make their move, launching an antiballistic weapon toward Kim's helicopter as Katy Perry's "Firework" plays. The movie doesn't attempt to get any deeper than this.

How North Korea found out about the movie is still a matter of Hollywood gossip. But before its release, on November 24, a hacker group called Guardians of Peace (GOP—get it?) started to leak confidential data and personal emails from the film studio. On that date, a "wiper attack" was launched by the Guardians on Sony, resulting in deleted data, disabled computers, and public disclosure of sensitive information that was eventually given to reporters. Employees came into work and saw images of red skeletons signed "GOP" (a pretty great pun), and eventually 70 percent of Sony's computers had been disabled. Sony staff were reduced to using pens and paper. Meanwhile, the public was able to enjoy details about executive salaries, ideas for future Sony films, releases of films yet to be distributed, and personal discussions and gossip about actors and public figures. Eventually, the hackers were able to erase the computer's entire infrastructure. In not-so-technical terms, they had devoured the network.

The hack wasn't just an embarrassment. It also reached national security status. The GOP hackers threatened terrorist attacks at cinemas where the film was set to be screened. In response, many US movie theaters decided not to show it, and Sony canceled both the formal premiere and eventually the mainstream release, only making the film available for digital download. The government put its intelligence efforts into identifying the culprit: after a thorough review of the software and networks, they determined it was sponsored directly from the North Korean government.[11]

Years later, I had the opportunity to interview Jim Clapper for this book. Clapper was the director of National Intelligence, the leader of the US intelligence community, during the Sony hack.[12] He remains the longest-serving director. With the benefit of hindsight, Clapper was circumspect about what happened during the Sony attack. "There's only two conditions in life," he told me. "There's a policy success or an intelligence failure. There's no other condition in life. I've found and observed that it's very hard for people to get their head around something that's never happened to them."[13] I like his terminology.

Everybody thinks security is fiendishly difficult, but it really isn't. This is often because the threat isn't all that smart either. There was no North Korean Einstein who devised the hack. The movie was regarded in North Korea as an insult to the ruling Kim family, who are accorded almost semidivine status. That fact was widely known. Sony assumed that it wasn't at risk, that it was impervious to crisis. This is wishful thinking and wrong. And it ignored history: Sony had been targeted multiple times before. Even before the film was announced publicly, there were specific threats against it, but that didn't seem to move Sony to take additional security precautions.

Sony didn't view itself as a potential target; it thought there would be no surprises. And thus, the company made no special efforts to prepare itself for an attack, let alone look for one. The intrusion went undetected for three weeks as the North Koreans gathered sensitive data. It began through easy points of entry, protected with passwords like "12345" and "ABCDE." These easily targeted passwords brought the whole system down and led to a corporate crisis and a national security issue. It defies basic *cyber hygiene*—the horrible phrase to describe commonsense policies to ensure that there are layered defenses—that an entire global entertainment company could be so easily penetrated.[14] It only makes sense if the company's leadership couldn't get their heads around it.

THE DISASTER DANCE

As part of getting our heads around the inevitability of disasters, it is necessary to understand the operational fundamentals of what happens at boom. My goal is to make this whole scary disaster response effort both more transparent and more pressing for all of us. There should be no more experts, or put another way, we are all experts. So a basic primer on what happens during an emergency response when a disaster occurs can provide some transparency. What does it mean to say a response has been activated? There will be differences in emphasis and titles, but the structure of disaster management is roughly the same universally in both the public and private sector. Its foundation is called the Incident Command System (ICS). The details of ICS are generally well known in the first responder world, lesser known everywhere else. I have long believed it is essential that

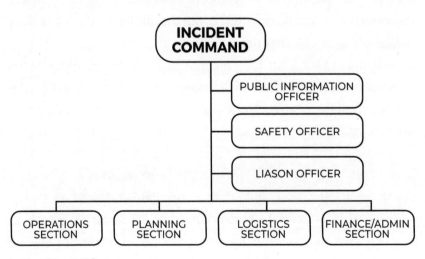

Incident Command System.

anybody in a leadership position understand this process. Again, it isn't so we all become first responders, but that we are smart enough to manage the next disasters.

ICS is a coordinated, hierarchical template that organizes people and resources for a large-scale response to a crisis. It allows for leadership—with an incident commander—to task key divisions in logistics, planning, and finance to be ready for an immediate reaction.[15] The ICS model was first adopted by firefighters in the 1970s as fires became larger and responders needed the capacity to expand over time and geography. As they confronted wildfires and factory-wide fires, it became unsustainable to maintain the same processes that had guided firefighting when a house or a building burned. The beauty of the model is that it has a plug-and-play aspect; firefighters from New York can be flown into a raging event in California and know exactly what to do.[16] That universality has been key in a world where crises are not limited in time and geography.

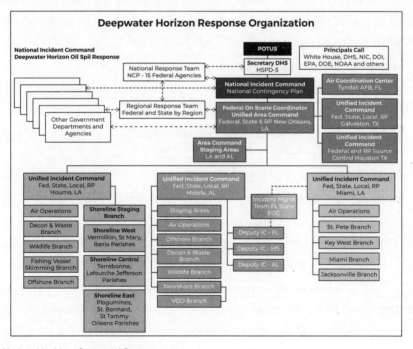

National Incident Command System.

ICS is easy to learn; it is worth the few hours of effort. There are online courses for managers, the media, and politicians so that they can understand the basics of what is happening in the field operationally. This chart shows the framework. It is self-explanatory; again, not rocket science. It is organized even if it looks like madness from the outside. But it can still get complex. The ICS system created—in real time—during the 2010 BP oil spill, as the spill expanded over days across Texas, Louisiana, Alabama, Mississippi, and Florida, grew with the scale of the disaster so it ended up looking like this.

Still, it has the same contours. The ICS template has survived because it is flexible. Look closely; it is pretty much the same as its simple cousin. The necessity of this disaster dance isn't just that it coordinates different aspects of crisis response, but that it also allows for adaptation in real time. When those in the disaster field talk about training and exercises to prepare for an event or a crisis, they are just talking shorthand for working through an ICS and what would happen if anything went wrong. They figure out how they would move resources, expand capacity, or seek assistance. While directed by a framework, they try to anticipate what might unfold.

This technical, operational know-how isn't the beginning and end. It is just essential to recognize what a typical response looks like and the foundations that guide it. The challenges laid out ahead are about how leaders can better recognize, communicate, and adapt these responses in a world of crisis after crisis. ICS exists to help organize responders because we know the disaster is coming. But that is all. It is agnostic about the who, what, why, and how.

And, of course, the when. ICS response is not self-executing. Somebody in charge has to activate it. Timing is everything with crisis response. Defining the boom at the right place—the MCAS failure, for example, rather than when the plane goes down—allows an institution to focus more quickly on activating and adapting to the crisis it is in and the right-of-boom investments that will limit and delay the consequences.

Back to COVID-19, when timing was everything. The pandemic officially began on January 17, 2020, when the World Health Organization (WHO) announced that the disease could no longer be contained. Though it may have been a little late, the boom was announced publicly. The WHO's assessment meant that all countries had received some warning that they needed to prepare their nations for what was likely to occur; the boom had happened.

The US government's response to the COVID-19 virus was a case study in the capacity for denial to lead to greater tragedy. When the president was notified of a novel virus in Wuhan, China, and its potential to become a global pandemic, he downplayed the risks to the American public and failed to unleash the tremendous powers of a federal bureaucracy that could have responded in real time. Specifically, from January to March 2020, before there was massive community spread throughout the United States, the administration squandered the response time. By April, the United States had its first nationwide disaster, encompassing all fifty states.[17] This meant that every state had activated its emergency response system and was working to deal with the pandemic through its ICS structure. It wasn't obvious from the outside, but for the first time in US history, all states were in incident command mode. But April was too late.

Throughout 2020, the president alternatively deluded the public, waged war with governors who were trying to respond, failed to execute on a plan that would provide personal protective equipment and other resources, and played politics with public health initiatives such as masking. Was the president scared? Overwhelmed? Unable to do his job? Did he not care? Whatever his motivation, he acted as if ignoring the virus would make it go away.[18]

I was teaching my crisis management course that spring semester. I remember the first class in January when I told the students that we would use the unfolding (and understated) "COVID issue" as a real-world example. Each week that month and the next, COVID became

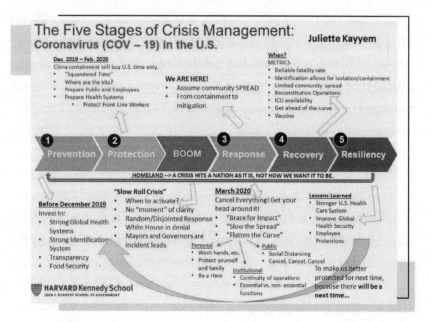

Produced by the author.

more of a focus. The class and I were adrift; so I tried to ground them, and myself, in the process by updating my chart—the "boom" one described in the introduction—so that we could all brace for what was ahead and what they could expect in the worst-case scenario. I got my head around it because I didn't know what else to do. By March, the students would soon be dismissed from campus, and I would be teaching remotely.

The chart held up pretty well (though I noticed later that I failed to mention masking), though more detailed and complicated than a generic left- and right-of-boom graphic. In it, I highlight different phases of crisis management—prevention, protection, response, recovery, and resiliency. Looking back on the chart a year and a half into the pandemic, it made me furious that someone with little specialist knowledge could have recognized that there was no tuning out, that this slow-roll crisis required someone in charge to say that we were in it and the only way forward was through it with eyes wide open.

Instead, the government of the most capable nations on earth said and did almost nothing during those initial, vital weeks.

What did the administration think would happen? This is ultimately what was unforgivable about our national response. It wasn't that the president didn't stop the virus. It was a global pandemic; there were going to be deaths. It was that he didn't focus on consequence minimization, that the measure of success might be 100,000 lives lost instead of more than 750,000 and counting. That is how we must measure victory in a recurring-disaster world. Instead, Trump let it roll over us like the plague.

Shift to the left. The COVID-19 boom happened in January and February 2020. It was undeniable; it didn't require massive community spread to recognize it. And if we had defined it as such, our response to minimize the consequences would have begun then. We wouldn't have squandered so much time. We might have made masks available, put into place social distancing efforts, and spoken to the public so that everyone might better prepare. Step one in any leadership role is to define the right side of the boom early enough and get our heads around it. By assuming the boom, then the either/or fallacy of success can be rejected. "Yes, something bad, catastrophically bad, could happen, and I am going to do everything possible to stop it from doing so. But let's get real. It will happen. And when it does, I still have a responsibility to make things better, or less bad, than if I pretended like it couldn't happen." This is what my fictional hero tells herself every day.

SETTING THE CONDITIONS OF "SUCCESS"

Boeing. Sony. The United States government. So many others. These aren't (always) stupid companies or institutions led by careless leaders. Yet smart companies and careful leaders also experience crises. Figuring out the reasons why something bad happens may lead us to understand how to better protect ourselves. But in an era of disaster after disaster, the clearer solution is a simple takeaway, in Jim Clapper's words: "The assumption should be that if you have a connection to the internet, you are inherently insecure. You're vulnerable. So assume you are going to get attacked. And what's important is how do you recover from that?"[19]

I didn't notice it when we spoke, but after reading his transcript, the magnitude of what Clapper was telling me was clear. The former leader of America's intelligence community, an entity that exists to stop attacks from happening, to predict, to protect, was urging a safety apparatus to prepare for the inevitability of an attack. Get your head around it. The measure of success was how best we could recover from it. "Never again"? Not anymore. Clapper isn't buying it either.

We are all crisis managers now: at home, at work, in the world. Certainly, we can delegate some of the details and technical know-hows such as the specifics of managing an ICS. But by anticipating a move to the right side of the boom, there will be more emphasis on how to minimize the consequences. Everybody can do it. "I divide up leadership into two types: crisis and noncrisis. I don't think there's a generic leadership. I think there's leadership in two settings. Those are two big different settings, two very different skills," Nassir Ghaemi, the author of *A First-Rate Madness: Uncovering the Links Between Leadership and Madness*, described to me.[20]

"Good leadership," said Nassir, "is simple. It is knowing that the crisis is coming."[21]

It seems so obvious now, in the context of the disaster that unfolded, that Boeing was careless, profit hungry, negligent. But something happened along the way—at Boeing, Sony, and elsewhere—where the safety mission became one of future planning, not daily routine. They never accepted the mission but instead wished away the potential harm as something that belonged in the future or was so inconsistent with their core competency—well-built planes in Boeing's case, movies in Sony's case—that the flashing warning lights were never viewed as an immediate stop sign.

The question isn't whether the blindness is fixable after the fact—institutions can learn their lessons, after all—but whether it was acknowledged beforehand. If you knew the devil was returning again and again, it would seem less feasible to structure your planning with a Whac-A-Mole philosophy, thinking every bad event was a fluke. Ultimately, the fix isn't some logo or corporate cliché. It is a basic design feature that has to accept that the worst-case scenario is possible again and again. And again. What would you do then? You would still put planes in the air and bad movies on screen. But you would also make sure that you saw the crisis coming as early as possible, if only to prepare for it hitting its target. Disaster management doesn't begin when the bodies start to fall from the sky. Then it is too late.

In a study done during the pandemic, a group of scholars who research fear and anxiety tried to determine what kind of American was better prepared for COVID-19. They measured preparedness not just in terms of whether citizens had supplies and food in anticipation of lockdowns but also looked at psychological resiliency and people's capacity to adapt. Maybe, they thought, there is a unifying personality type that can help determine how best to be prepared and make it through.

"In this study, we found that people who watched a lot of zombie movies and other apocalyptic-type films reported feeling more prepared for the pandemic," researcher Coltan Scrivner told *Forbes* magazine.[22] He called it "morbid curiosity," the fascination with disasters and death. It turns out that those who think a lot about bad things that could happen (I fear I may be in this category) and have a certain amount of fixation with the right side of the boom are both stimulated to act early and more mentally prepared for the next unfolding disaster. Through movies and books, they had become more relaxed about anticipating the worst: it did not scare them; it motivated them and grounded them.

Get your head around it. Good leadership is knowing the crisis is coming. You are here.

CHAPTER TWO

WHAT'S THE WORD?

"Know What Your Fire Is Doing"

On August 5, 1949, a wildfire started at Mann Gulch, an area along the Upper Missouri River that flows through the Gates of the Mountain Wilderness at Helena National Forest in Montana. When the fire was reported, a team of fifteen smokejumpers was parachuted into the area to assist those at a nearby campground. There were high winds, and as the men began to approach the fire on foot, it suddenly became dangerously uncontrollable, increasing and expanding and blocking off any exits for them. They were compelled to return uphill to their landing area. It was there that a rare, but deadly, blowup occurred, the fire expanding more than three thousand acres in ten minutes. Twelve of the smokejumpers were killed. The fire was eventually extinguished on August 10, 1949.[1]

The fire itself started when lightning struck a tree and a forest ranger tried to put it out. Working initially for four hours by himself, the ranger realized he needed help. The smokejumpers were sent from Missoula, Montana, on a Douglas DC-3 to assist. The fire was on a 75 percent incline slope, making it more difficult to evade. The firefighters' single radio had failed, so communication was difficult; as the fire got more dangerous, a last-minute last-ditch effort to escape was likely misunderstood by some of the firefighters, and they would eventually perish.

Foreman Wagner "Wag" Dodge, trapped with several men, understood that he could not escape in time. He tried an act so bizarre it
has taken on mythic proportions: he lit a match to burn the grass in
front of him to better clear an escape area. Dodge wasn't planning to
run from the fire. He was planning to lie in the cleared area to let the
big fire burn around them. The other men would have none of it,
maybe first misunderstanding him and then, after seeing what he
was doing, deciding to try to escape. They would not make it. The folk
singer James Keelaghan would later write of Dodge's effort:[2]

> I don't know why, I just thought it. I don't know why, I just
>   thought it.
> I struck a match to waist-high grass, running out of time.
> Tried to tell them, "Step into this fire I set.
> We can't make it, this is the only chance you'll get."
> But they cursed me, ran for the rocks above instead.
> I lay face down and prayed above the cold Missouri waters.

In *Young Men and Fire*, author Norman Maclean revisits the tragedy
and examines the mistakes made. It is his story of Dodge that inspired
Keelaghan's song. Maclean's hope was that through the process of
understanding the mindset of the men during the incident, examining what they perceived in the moments of the disaster, their situational awareness, we might come to better understand what went
wrong. These lessons could help future firefighting efforts.

It was the fire that killed, but it was the wind—and assumptions
about wind—that was responsible. Maclean showed that the wind
was traveling downriver, to the north, and not upstream, which was
the norm. This troublesome wind would divide, then reunite in the
gulch itself, increasing the heat and fire and leading to the blowup.
That event would cause a significant change in the peril that the men
faced. Mainly, the surface fire, or the fire that was eating grass and

branches on the ground, soon became a crown fire, burning top branches, or the canopy.[3] Because the men were on a slope, the elevated fire rained down on them below.

Firefighting would change after that disaster. The Ten Standard Firefighting Orders were adopted to help avoid future catastrophes and improve capabilities to stop wildfires. Adopted in 1957, they are guidelines, similar to a checklist, that every firefighter knows and understands. They are in no particular order or prioritization, and their main focus is less about how to fight the fire and more about how to understand and communicate what the fire is doing. The list includes reminders to continually post lookouts when potential danger may be coming, to understand the expected behavior of the fire, to maintain prompt communications with your own and adjoining forces, and to "know what your fire is doing at all times."[4]

A fire is a natural disaster when awareness is key. In manmade horrors, mostly terrorism, we also talk in terms of awareness, but they are called intelligence failures. Investigators and congressional hearings try to unearth what clues might have been missed before the events that led to death or destruction. The January 6, 2021, attack on the Capitol was examined just for that reason, for example. What was known, and what wasn't known to the officers on the ground, will be studied for years to come. Politics aside, if the Capitol Police were caught completely off guard, even while others were sounding the bell as a mob walked to the building and eventually breached the entrance, somewhere along the way there was a gap in understanding and communication. But to call it an intelligence failure assumes that there was no intelligence to be had. That wasn't the case; many, including the Virginia FBI, had been warning of potential violence.[5] This is so often the truth in disaster management. The key challenge isn't that nothing was known, but that what was known wasn't acted on. "Know what your fire is doing at all times" is good advice as we prepare for the next boom.

WTW

Before there was a vaccine for smallpox, it raged through populations, killing young and old alike. Its symptoms ranged from mild rash to flu-like symptoms to, in at least 30 percent of those infected, death. Its name, describing the small blisters victims suffered, was in no way a reflection of its destructiveness; nothing about it was small. Outbreaks were not uncommon in America's early colonies and perhaps worst in dense, urban areas like Boston. In 1702 and 1703, a smallpox outbreak occurred in the New England city, and they were ill-prepared to address it. It could not be controlled. Government officials decided to take a unique approach to the disaster in front of them. In an effort to minimize panic and retain normalcy among residents, city leaders denied the reality of what was occurring. They hid what was happening from the public by prohibiting churches from ringing bells to memorialize the dead. Even as the death count steadily rose, the city forbade the bells.[6]

Smallpox is a disease transferred from human to human, so knowledge of its wide existence in a population is a fact that ought to be known to potentially vulnerable citizens. But the bells were silent. Without the bells tolling, Boston officials had hoped they could quietly move on. A silent bell, they thought, rang for no one.

Boston suffered through that outbreak. It could have ended at that, a tragedy lost to history, not even a footnote in the prerevolutionary era. But smallpox had additional plans. It next arrived by ship, a generation later, greeting a fresh Boston population ready to be infected. On April 22, 1721, a British passenger ship named the HMS *Seahorse* arrived from Barbados. On Spectacle Island in Boston Harbor, there was a customs' quarantine hospital intended for any person who may have been exposed. One sailor on the *Seahorse* soon showed symptoms of smallpox, but by the time it was discovered and he was in quarantine, he had infected nine other shipmen.[7] They fell ill in May, but by then it was too late; though they would be quarantined, they had already spread smallpox in the town. By 1722, over 8 percent of Boston's population had died. Churches would eventually hold only limited services in order to protect congregants. Their bells rang this time, however, and did not stop.

What were those earlier Boston officials thinking? The kindest explanation for their deceit is that they may have been trying to curb panic. The tolling bells were a constant reminder, like Edgar Allen Poe's tell-tale heart, of the city's failure to protect its citizens. In those times, however, the absence of the bells meant that the city residents had no clear sense of the magnitude of the harm. Maybe without the bells, leaders could convince residents that the outbreak was manageable, more like the flu than a deadly virus. Perhaps it would go away on its own accord, and the disaster would pass. Boston could return to normal. Smallpox, of course, could care less about the bells.

When we look at disasters with the benefit of hindsight, how they unfolded is already written. Times, places, events are quickly reported on, assessed, and understood. The failure to respond adequately, in real time, seems negligent or stupid in hindsight. But in real time, what is in fact happening is not so easily known. Information and disinformation, data, rumors, and suspicions all fight for focus in the moments of panic. Assuming we are on the verge of the boom moment, any institution, community, or individual will not seem overprepared to create structures that, essentially, capture WTW.

This is not a complicated acronym. I learned from one of my kids the initials WTW are for "What's the word?" He explained it to me after I expressed surprise, if not envy, that two minutes after he told me he didn't know what his plans were, he all of a sudden knew his plans. All that happened within those two minutes was a single text he sent out to his gang of friends: WTW? What's the word? Moments later, he knew, and off he went.

Preparation for recurring disasters requires knowledge of when and what is going on: WTW. That seems obvious to write but is often neglected in practice. We have not built up sufficient mechanisms to gather information as a disaster unfolds that can help drive our response, make it more effective, and minimize the consequences. We focus a lot on "intelligence failures" that could have prevented the harm from coming and less on how the crisis is unfolding and how to mitigate losses.

Situational awareness, or situation awareness (SA), is defined as the memorialization or record of events as they occur over time and location, what that data means, and how it prepares planners for future status, even if it is only hours away. It is a way first responders document what is happening and what needs to happen to respond at that moment; it also is predictive, attempting to document what may happen next and what will be needed.

It is essential for effective consequence management; its absence contributes to greater loss. Situational awareness is both about being ready, of course, and aligning capabilities to what the data and information is telling us so as to avoid a catastrophe. But such intelligence isn't just for preventative left-of-boom purposes. In a world in which we should anticipate harm, situational awareness describes the methods and processes in place to assess what is happening as the damage unfolds so a leader can best be prepared to minimize it.

Generally, there are three parts of any effective SA document or database. These templates can be created now; they don't require waiting for the disaster to unfold. The parts include the following: what is happening (perception); what it means (comprehension); and what may likely happen (projection). For consequence minimization purposes, leaders require mechanisms to know what the heck is happening (perception) so that resources can be focused to where they are needed (comprehension) and be moved to where they might be needed in the future (projection).

PERCEPTION	COMPREHENSION	PROJECTION
What is happening	What it means	What may likely happen

  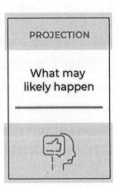

Situational awareness elements.

Left-of-boom awareness—risk assessments, intelligence reports—is not mutually exclusive from awareness while the event unfolds, after the boom. They are related. Reimagine the events leading to January 6, 2021. Had a serious effort been made to assess the threat ahead, not only would there have been a greater deployment of resources and personnel beforehand—I have long thought that the mere presence of the National Guard on Capitol Hill would have deterred most if not all of the insurrectionists—there would have been greater focus on creating a situational awareness capacity to assess real-time needs during that day. By understanding and acting on the pre-event information and intelligence, those who need to respond will have time to better situate themselves to limit the damage.

GENERAL OFFICER, BRIGHT IDEA

When a disaster occurs, everybody will have an opinion about how those handling the crisis suck. It is an accepted and understood reality by those who work in disaster management: everything sucks. A disaster, by definition, means that things are so miserable and horrible and seemingly unfixable that those who are leading a response can't possibly be doing anything right. In the military, the phenomenon of the outsider coming in, commenting with profound wisdom but little insight, is called a GOBI—a General Officer, Bright Idea. This is a way that soldiers make fun of generals and other high-ranking officials who walk into a situation and pontificate, like, "We really should fix this," as if nobody else had ever thought of that idea. Brilliant. We should really fix this.

Instead of looking at situational awareness as a term to describe the intelligence apparatus set up to prevent a bad thing from happening, we also have to establish mechanisms that capture what is happening in the disaster in real time as it unfolds. Information must be reliable, quick, in the hopes that responsible leadership can adapt immediately.

Time and again, I am struck by how often key players find it difficult to understand events as they play out in real time. They seem caught off guard, as if they never imagined that the boom would come. Even the most sophisticated companies can get caught with little transparency. In 2018, hundreds of passengers were stranded on a parked JetBlue plane for up to ten and a half hours at JFK Airport because of icy weather and gate congestion. Exasperated passengers sat within sight of the terminal without food, an adequate restroom, or a reasonable explanation as to why they were not moving. What happened? CEO David Neeleman, who would announce a $30 million investment in disruption management after the disaster played out in real time on cable news, admitted he was "humiliated and mortified" by the events. The breakdown was not one of capacity but one of communication. Neeleman believed that his team had asked airport officials for help to offload the plane when no such request had been made. The communication breakdown meant that Neeleman thought one thing, the airport another, and his team a third. The solution was an easy one if only they had built consistent situational awareness. The result: a $30 million apology tour.

It didn't help that it was Valentine's Day. JetBlue was completely dependent on a reservation system controlled by a dispersed workforce, so when the expected rainstorm turned to ice, there was no surge capacity when thousands of passengers needed to rebook at once. Indeed, the communication that made Neeleman aware of the breakdown wasn't some sophisticated system of data management. It was an angry phone call from the pilot on the plane, who told him passengers were hungry and thirsty, toilets were overflowing, and flight attendants could no longer keep passengers safe and comfortable.

Disasters, generically, are predictable: the devil will come. But after the boom, they unfold in quite unique ways. The only constant is that the boom has been breached. Everybody is pissed. Some are horrified, others traumatized, some outraged. And for leaders in big and small enterprises, let alone at home, this can cause defensiveness or an inability to look directly into the sun no matter how dangerous or damaging. Thus, there is a tendency to think the complainers are just that, naysayers and nonexperts who have no idea of the extent of the situation. But sometimes, just sometimes, there is wisdom in the noise. And leaders need to have a way to hear the noise, listen, absorb, and adapt to it. But first, they have to capture it.

Hopefully, there are basic structures already in place to do this. For multinational corporations, they'll have employees on the ground who are providing real-time information. Governments will have first responders or law enforcement at the scene. Databases or web services, like Slack, are often used to provide information in real time. But delineating good information from bad information is tricky in a disaster. Disasters are phenomena in which there is so much noise, it is difficult to process. How to get live information? Why not just turn on the TV? Sometimes that works. Twitter? Maybe. Don't ignore those platforms, but the complainer—a civilian GOBI—may always get the limelight, may have the most followers, but it is often unclear whether he or she has a lot of knowledge. The blowhards on Twitter—the conservative television commentator Piers Morgan is not, in fact, an emergency manager—who take nuggets of information, or waves of disinformation, to relate to their millions of followers are not viable guides during a disaster. Volume is not often a good metric. And big things, really big things, can be missed if the mechanisms for information gathering and communication are not nurtured beforehand.

An example is the levee breach in New Orleans during Hurricane Katrina in 2005. After Katrina passed through New Orleans, there was a quiet period when it seemed—maybe, just maybe—the city had survived the worst. Katrina, after all, was a Category 3 hurricane by the time it hit landfall, not a devastating Category 5. Stability, it seemed, could be possible. But then the trickles became a flood.

It would be more than twelve hours before the White House and Secretary of Homeland Security Michael Chertoff were notified of the breach and overflow. Yet anyone actually in New Orleans would have known by then, if not before.[8] The gap in time is explained by the fact that the federal government was completely dependent on its own resources for postdisaster awareness, and somehow they didn't have enough capability on the ground to figure out the obvious. In what may have been the worst timing for a cable news hit, Chertoff—who had not been notified of the breach through his own system of awareness, a complicated federal awareness apparatus known as the National Operations Center—seemed unaware the levees had been breached as the news feed itself showed the overflow. New Orleanians were screaming, literally from the rooftops, that their city was flooding. The information Chertoff was receiving from the federal teams on the ground was just too slow, too high level, too alienated from what was in fact happening. Response time matters: any delay of that magnitude costs lives. The federal government's insistence that all was well also gave false assurances to the public that they could stay put. The noise was telling the federal government the waters had come, but they weren't listening.

WISDOM IN THE NOISE, AND SILENCE

Noise, though, doesn't have to be loud. In one well-known instance of successful adaptation of information, the noise was actually the silence. It was San Francisco mayor London Breed who, it seemed to many watching, hastily set rules to promote social distancing and stay-at-home orders in the early weeks of March 2020. They were described as "unprecedented," though the rest of the country would soon follow.[9] Her "noise," it turned out, was the Chinese New Year celebration that was attended annually by the city's Chinese American residents. But the 2020 celebration was different. On February 10 of that year, the events were noticeably less crowded. Few turned out. Some festivities were canceled. Had Breed followed established awareness protocols for her city, she would have missed the silent noise as the federal government was telling her everything was fine. But it wasn't, and she knew it.[10]

Her curiosity may be the modern-day equivalent of the 1892 Sherlock Holmes "Silver Blaze" mystery. Author Sir Arthur Conan Doyle wrote of the disappearance of a famous racehorse and the death of its trainer the night before a big competition. The detective is asked to solve the case and finds wisdom in the silence more than in any noise. Holmes tells another detective at Scotland Yard that he found the behavior of the "dog in the night-time" curious. The other detective says that there is no evidence that the dog did anything that night. "That was the curious incident," Holmes explained. The dog's silence meant that the culprit was known to the quiet canine. The search was then easily solved.[11]

In 2020, the Chinese New Year festivities were also quiet. The mayor deployed her teams to assess what was going on. It turns out Chinese American citizens had plenty of family members who were living through COVID-19's impact in China, a few weeks ahead of us in the pandemic. The San Francisco residents were scared for their loved ones in China, and they were scared about what was likely to occur here. They told city officials that this coronavirus was different, that their families were telling them it was different. They did not feel comfortable partying in early March 2020.

Believe what you see and also what you don't. Listen to what is being said in whatever way it is being said. The ability to capture what is happening is essential because, often, the noise is correct; it has wisdom. It isn't just a bunch of GOBIs or cranks. The noise and quiet can help any of us avoid getting trapped in the land of wishful thinking. Listen for the noise.

This notion of expanding our ability to absorb more information rather than less can seem inconsistent with a sense that noise is antifact, antivalidation. "Noise" is often seen as bad, disruptive, and random. It is deemed unreliable, much like a bias that leads people to act on racial or gender stereotypes. But noise can also be helpful, exposing impacts that aren't being captured by standard procedures. We must leave ourselves open to the noise and what it is telling us.

This dilemma—how to manage and understand noise—is addressed in a recent book by Daniel Kahneman, Olivier Sibony, and Cass Sunstein called, appropriately, *Noise: A Flaw in Human Judgment*. Their argument is that noise is an "unwanted variability, and if something is unwanted, it should probably be eliminated."[12] In the book, they argue that too much noise in systems—randomness not relevant to the decision maker—can lead to bad decision-making, just like any bias.

The notion is appealing as a way of confronting inexplicable divergences in decision-making, from insurance claims to criminal justice sentencing, that can't solely be explained by a bias. But if the goal of reducing noise is to promote some objective judgment for better accuracy, that assumes a level of stability and number-driven analysis that may not exist in a disaster or crisis. The examples the authors use to assess the impact of noise, such as in the medical or legal professions, are examinations of datasets and behaviors over long periods of time. In a crisis, time to respond is truncated, accuracy is measured differently, and minimizing losses may be the best that can be done.

Also, by opening ourselves up to the noise, we can hear the voices of those who may not have the same power or resources as those with megaphones (or large Twitter followings). Unlike other fields, such as public health or medicine or law, where conclusive evidence exists to show how those institutions are systematically biased, consequence management often works in bulk. Disaster managers don't think in terms of individuals, per se, but generic survivors or victims. They don't have clients or patients. And working with such metrics can seem crude, even unforgiving. "Go Big or Stay Home" is a motto often heard by emergency managers, meaning just surge everything until it is time to go home or resources aren't needed. Yet these measurements can hide gaps in equity or fairness that are essential for effective consequence management. A nation that is successfully vaccinating, for example, can't say that it is successful if the campaign is missing minority or underserved communities. So situational awareness also has to be granular, even noisy, enough to capture the kinds of inequities that may surface if resources are guided by unequal standards.

THE CHEAP SEATS IN THE BACK

The 1986 *Challenger* shuttle disaster is one of the most studied disasters for how an entire institution, well aware of the risks ahead, let ego and politics silence the warning signs. The accident was later determined to be caused by a destabilized O-ring that held the exterior engine but was unable to withstand the freezing temperatures before launch. Yet the O-ring problem was not a mystery, it turns out. It wasn't even a secret.

The average American might have thought that the *Challenger* disaster was just the consequence of dangerous space travel. Inevitable, tragic, but in an odd way understandable. But in all the analysis of the *Challenger,* it turns out the concerns of an impending disaster were being articulated. The problem was that the greatest gadfly, the guy who knew that the *Challenger* should not fly and said so on one of the last preflight check-in phone calls, was an outsider who wasn't let in. He was noise, a mere contractor, not even an employee, to NASA.

The story of engineer and whistleblower Allan McDonald is a story of a man who knew too much.[13] McDonald was head of a booster rocket project working on the *Challenger.* He worked at the engineering firm Morton Thiokol but had been contracted to NASA to work on the shuttle. At the Kennedy Space Center that morning, January 27, 1986, he watched a shuttle he knew should not fly explode into thin air. The day before, he had refused—absolutely refused—to sign the official form required to be submitted before flight. "And I made the smartest decision I ever made in my lifetime," McDonald said. "I refused to sign it. I just thought we were taking risks we shouldn't be taking."[14]

McDonald was a pretty normal guy: smart, committed, and worried what his refusal would mean for his family and work. He knew the O-rings would not hold. On the morning of the launch, ice formed at the launchpad and put stress on the tiles that were not made for conditions below fifty degrees Fahrenheit. McDonald had tested the shuttle's machinery at fifty-three degrees and measured subsequent O-ring elasticity. In the colder conditions, the explosive fuel burning inside the rockets would not be contained. "If anything happens to this launch, I wouldn't want to be the person that has to stand in front of a board of inquiry to explain why we launched," he once noted.[15] He was the outsider, strenuously opposing the launch with his team of Thiokol engineers. But throughout, he was "in the cheap seats in the back" and was eventually overruled by Thiokol executives after NASA officials pressed them for a signature. It was easy for NASA to sideline him.

THE DEVIL NEVER SLEEPS

McDonald's courage went further. His famous moment before the independent commission investigating the explosion is the stuff movies are made of. Listening to NASA's deception after deception at the hearing, McDonald stood up. He was not a witness. He was not scheduled to be a witness and was just watching in the spectator area. He got to his feet. "So . . . I said I think this presidential commission should know that Morton Thiokol was so concerned, we recommended not launching below 53 degrees Fahrenheit. And we put that in writing and sent that to NASA," he related from the audience. It was only at that moment that the investigation started to examine the O-rings, McDonald's efforts to stop the launch, and NASA's cover-ups. Nonetheless, McDonald was demoted and was brought back only after political intervention. In some sort of vindication, he was eventually put in charge of redesigning the O-ring booster rocket joints.

Of course, the issue of the *Challenger* disaster is so much bigger than McDonald's status as a contractor, the guy in the cheap seats. NASA was under tremendous pressure to get a teacher up in space for the first time; Christa McAuliffe, a mother, was a household name by then. The State of the Union was the day after the launch, and there was a political incentive to get the shuttle in the air so President Ronald Reagan could speak of it. The agency was hell-bent on mission accomplished. McDonald felt that his status hindered his ability to stop the launch. He recalls how he was always in the back seat, easily overruled with no power to shift the institution he loved so dearly. He was just noise.

This isn't to say every outsider has validity. In an age of disinformation, as we saw throughout the pandemic, science and reality must reign. It is, however, a warning that the way we collect and assess information in a crisis must be flexible enough to absorb and reflect on the noise. Institutions should look at the way they collect information and ensure it covers the range of impacted communities: employees, customers, students, citizens, contractors, and those who may not have the power and thus say nothing at all. They'll know a lot. Not every crank is correct, but sometimes he or she can see the flashing red lights before anybody else.

AVOID CASSANDRA'S CURSE

WTW isn't just about what information is collected during a crisis. It is also about what information is conveyed. The next step is to use information as a guide through the postboom madness, misery, and fear. The best lessons for that come not from Sherlock Holmes detective stories or a NASA contractor's heroic efforts but from Greek mythology.

The prophet Cassandra is mostly known for her warning of disasters, her knowledge of the future, and the damage that would befall her people and her captors. However, she wasn't a mere prophet; she was a cursed one. She was doomed to see the future, but also doomed to the indignity that nobody would believe her. She was all-knowing; she had the best situational awareness of the doom to come, but nobody would listen. As memorialized by Homer and Euripides and others, her knowledge of future deaths, murder, and captivity—and her attempts to warn others—would always fall on deaf ears.[16]

Her knowledge wasn't the mere gossip of a teenager. She tried to tell her Greek neighbors that the kingdom of Troy's gift of a grand Trojan horse was not all it was cut out to be. But the curse that she would never be believed was made worse because it was a curse that gave her knowledge but no way to relate it, to warn. This take on an old Greek myth was described in NPR's podcast *Hidden Brain* based on the work of University of Pennsylvania professor Emily Wilson. She relates how Cassandra's failures to provide adequate and effective awareness condemned her to the ignominy of being famous for mostly being ignored.[17]

For us to better communicate the information that we have so that others can be guided by it after the boom, her curse is a cautionary tale and a helpful guide. The curse was cruel because it involved multiple elements, frustrating her success. Her "failed attempts to warn those around her can give us insights into how warnings are heard, when they are taken seriously, and when they are acted upon," explained Wilson.[18] The three factors that constituted the elements of the curse itself were that her messages were too opaque, she had no formal authority to get her message out (much like McDonald of *Challenger* infamy), and what she was saying was too outside the realm of possibility for people to take her seriously.

Take Cassandra's warning to her captor, King Agamemnon of Mycenae, that his wife was having an affair and was going to kill him one night.[19] She tried to alert him through analogy and generalizations. Her words were too coy for him to understand the message. She needed to give a clear statement of what was going to happen. Her status as the "other"—a young woman, captive—also doomed her warning because it meant that she was viewed with some skepticism, as if she was just background noise. And, as if invoking the notion of getting his "head around it," as Wilson describes: "He (the King) wants to think of himself as a strong, triumphant city sacker. And he is only going to process the info that confirms that belief about

Overcoming Cassandra's Curse:

>> Speak Directly

>> Find Ways to Capture the Noise

>> Make the Improbable Familiar

himself. And he is going to ignore all the signs . . . that might suggest that that reality is not the only reality."[20] In the end, Cassandra's vision was true, and King Agamemnon was killed.

I use this reframing of the ancient Cassandra curse because it helps clarify present-day disasters. This may seem dated in an age of misinformation and social media manipulation, but the only way to counter the lies is to have complete mastery of the truth as it is understood at the moment it is being told—and then to repeat it again and again. The third part of the curse is that Cassandra was explaining events that seemed too improbable to the listeners. But if we can accept that a disaster is probable, not rare, then nothing will seem beyond the possible.

The lessons from her failures can help to create a better situational awareness in times of crisis. It takes an investment to counter the three parts of the curse that plagued Cassandra: speak directly, find ways to capture the noise, and believe that the improbable can be possible, that what is in fact happening—a disaster whose success will be measured in whether fewer people will die or less harm will be done—is happening. An animating theme of consequence minimization efforts is that leadership cannot wish away the possibility that the doom is already here. The guy in the cheap seats may have something important to say about that.

NUMBERS AND HOPE

Effective situational awareness will drive decision makers to two key needs in managing and limiting the impact of a disaster: basic data to guide response and an empathetic acknowledgment that things, indeed, are in peril but will get better. Two words: numbers and hope. Those who look to us for guidance—whether we are a CEO, a government official, a teacher, a parent—need to know what is happening in the moment and how we can make it better, or less crappy, tomorrow.

Often, situational awareness is presented as a single document that can help people visualize the numbers and then move resources. It highlights the numbers first and then what to make of those numbers to guide the days to come. Simple, clear, without emotion. The military often calls this BLUF: Bottom Line Up Front. Just the facts, easily accessible. Without continuing awareness that is adapting to the situation on the ground, there will be no bottom line, just a lot of chaos. Cut to the chase: What's the damage done? For those in disaster management, we can often do that in quantifiable terms: How many dead, injured, impacted? What is the number of resources being deployed, or planned, or en route? How long will it be this way, and how long until it gets better? That last part is the *hope* part. This simple two-word process, numbers and hope, should guide all of our communications for when the boom comes. Harm will be minimized if we can have a better understanding of what is occurring to guide the response and efforts for the hours, days, weeks that might follow.

We have become quite sophisticated with our left-of-boom awareness. Intelligence reports and law enforcement bulletins tell agencies what criminal or terror threats may be out there. The National Weather Service gives us a sense, in order to better prepare, that hurricanes or tornadoes are coming. Buoys in water tell us if a tsunami is coming. New technology is giving residents even a few seconds warning about earthquakes. Even after COVID, there is a movement to build a strong early-alert system for potential pandemics so that we aren't caught so flat-footed and can make decisions earlier and better—and prepare supply chains in anticipation of a public health crisis.[21]

We can become just as sophisticated in our postboom knowledge. If we can build a better capacity for consequence minimization, for example, a simple family phone tree to a complex logistics supply-chain chart, then managing a response and how those numbers get better, smaller, or bigger, depending on the crisis at hand, is easier. Situational awareness isn't just about knowing what is happening at that moment in time; it is also about knowing how to get to the next day. Numbers and hope. Or maybe better said, there is no hope without numbers. Crisis response will otherwise just seem like Whac-A-Mole.

Any institution, big or small, can build a communications system that absorbs and processes information successfully during a crisis, now. Solving these awareness challenges will better prepare us to minimize the consequences of a disaster. Information is relevant not just for the premonition but also for when it goes unheeded and the results are calamitous. Don't "other" information. Our comfort zone has to be gloom and doom. This rather admittedly dire information flow has to be embraced, accepted, if there is going to be any chance for it to be acted upon. Otherwise, no amount of planning or preparation will matter, as you'll just be sitting there letting the waters overflow the levee.

The challenge ahead isn't that the news might be bad and consequential, only whether we have established information-gathering efforts to ensure we know just how bad and consequential so we can do something about it. I am clearly a big fan of processes. Or let's say I find it inexcusable when people are caught flat-footed when they could have created valuable systems beforehand. Not everything can be solved by process, but it surely minimizes the panic during those initial minutes, hours, and days after a disaster. When a situation has been trained and tested to withstand or assume certain demands of a disaster, decision-making becomes more accurate. And to make the correct decisions, we must understand where the wisdom is in the noise. Two key processes can be established before the devil, inevitably, arrives.

First, establish a process of information gathering that will be triggered and followed through the entire crisis; it is a "battle rhythm" because it should be consistent and predictable. Again, because none of this should come as a surprise—the disasters are no longer random and rare—this can be done now. We don't need to know what, in fact, will happen, only that everyone will want to know what the hell is happening when it does. Sophisticated press offices know this is key, so they have to be key to internal management as well. They recognize the need to get information out in a consistent manner; police departments will regularly end a press conference saying, "We'll be back in three hours," or "Tomorrow morning, we will have more details."

This is often called a situation report, or SITREP, a process used frequently in the military during World War II. The infographic on Hurricanes Eta and Iota is a good example. Because agility is so essential during any disruption, information needs to be assessed quickly so that good decisions can be made as the environment changes. Leaders can prepare for this by training how to get better information using the SITREP process. A good SITREP not only includes the situation, actions taken, and actions to be completed, but also provides the issues and risks that need to be decided for tomorrow. An effective SITREP presents the issues that are likely to come up—say, for example, a shortage in the supply chain—and other potential failures in the future.

From the SITREP, the content of the battle rhythm for those who have to act can be determined and the pace set. It can be an hourly or daily email (same time each time), an all-hands meeting (same time each time), a Zoom briefing (same time each time), a way to fill the vacuum of fear and worry that is too often addressed by gossip or misinformation. A mastery of the facts is essential as it creates an open forum for structure, response, and a willingness to listen. As part of any planning, a system for situational awareness can be put into place beforehand and practiced. During a disaster, what would you want to know? Everything, of course, but what would you really need to know? Most organizations will know the answer now, before the boom comes.

Second, the awareness needs to be shared with all relevant parties. There is no "need to know"—the excuse within the intelligence agency

Pan American Health Organization · World Health Organization · Americas

December 2 - 5pm

HIGHLIGHTS

- **Honduras:** 414 health facilities have reported damage, of which, 120 health facilities are reported inoperative, 27 health facilities are collapsed and 12 report damage to cold chain equipment. Additionally, 99 health facilities report health personnel directly affected, complicating the continuity of health services. Approximately 2 million people have limited or no access to health services due to damage to the health services network, of which at least 500,000 have health needs. Furthermore, around 94,000 people remain in shelters, decreasing 81,000 since last week.

- **Guatemala:** 206 health facilities have reported damage, including: 79 in Alta Verapaz, 13 in Izabal, 36 in Quiche, 65 in Huehuetenango and 13 in Peten. No major health facility has reported damages. Furthermore, around 30,000 people remain in 317 shelters, decreasing 2,000 since last week. It is estimated the health sector requires at least USD$ 2 million to restore the operational functions of its service network in the five most affected departments (Alta Verapaz, Quiché, Petén, Izabal and Huehuetenango).

- **Colombia:** Providencia reports 1 health facility completely damaged and non-operative. Medical teams were deployed, mental health first aid has been provided and a field emergency hospital has been installed including outpatient services, emergency rooms with isolation capacity, and clinical lab. Furthermore, around 800 people remain in shelters.

SITUATION IN NUMBERS

2 hurricanes
Impacted the Central America region in November: Eta and Iota

Affected
>9M [1,2,3,4,5,6]

Deaths
#205 [1,2,3,4,5]

Damaged
#716 [1,2,5]

Missing
#113 [1,2,5]

Evacuated
>1M [1,2,3,4,5,6]

Sources:
1. CONRED report December 2 - Guatemala
2. PAHO PWR Update December 1 - Honduras
3. Govt of Panama report November 16
4. Govt of El Salvador December 2
5. PAHO PWR Sitrep December 1 - Colombia
6. PAHO PWR Sitrep November 19 - Costa Rica

Figure 1: La Lima, one of the most affected municipalities in Honduras
Source: PAHO Honduras

Figure 2: Inoperative health facility in Yoro, Honduras.
Source: PAHO Honduras

1

Example of a situational report, with permission from the WHO and PAHO.

that information should only be circulated to the inner circle. It's the complete opposite for right of the boom; information needs to be shared because everyone has the potential to help. In the same way our process to learn about information—listen to the noise and the silence, those not at the table, the folks in the cheap seats—needs to become more inclusive, we also need to disperse it in a more inclusive fashion.

I remember encountering the necessity of better situational awareness, and how it can better align operational decisions, during the BP oil spill. During that very long summer, the government's main focus was on supporting states and governors who, pursuant to the legal framework of the Oil Pollution Act, were the points of contact for the federal response. We, the US, had all the data, and we were sharing that data with the state leads. Over time, we had perfected it. There was a morning phone call, every morning, for more than one hundred days, at nine fifteen with the five impacted states—Texas, Louisiana, Alabama, Mississippi, and Florida—where we disclosed what we were seeing, the impact on each state, and what resources we were deploying. The numbers gave hope, or at least one would have hoped.

The problem was that we were working off a playbook built after the *Exxon Valdez* spill in 1989. Then, the oil tanker bound for Long Beach, California, hit a reef in Prince William Sound's Bligh Reef and spilled ten million gallons of crude oil. The cleanup and controversy resulted in a new law, the Oil Pollution Act, which required companies to pay for cleanup. But the law, based on the Exxon spill, limited our focus on the states. Exxon spilled, after all, in one state, without impacting a major population, before cable news, and with a known amount of oil that was discharged. The dynamics of the Gulf politics were different by magnitudes.[22]

Consequentially, the numbers weren't being shared beyond the governor's offices, who wanted to control all the information. This meant that the local jurisdictions—the counties, towns, and cities; the mayors and county commissioners; and parish presidents—were not part of any structured information flow. The feds weren't telling them; the states weren't telling them. They were out of the loop, and that hurt our operational response and those leaders' desire to empower others. We had failed to create an open network that would not only intake information (the noise) but also provide the path forward (the wisdom).

I was walking one day in a parish in Louisiana. Maybe there had just been a meeting or one of the hundreds of community outreach events done that summer. The parish president came running up to me. I was an easy target, serving as a representative of the Obama administration and the head of the government's outreach efforts. He looked upset, not angry, more frustrated, if anything. He told me he was "embarrassed." There were many words used that summer, but *embarrassed* was a new one. I had not anticipated it at all.

His particular focus was on something called in situ burnings, which is just a fancy way of describing the lighting of the oil on the ocean surface so it burns away before coming to shore. That day, we had decided and notified the states that we wouldn't be doing any burnings because of an uptick in the wind, which meant that the fumes could drift ashore and harm residents. It was a smart calculation if you knew why we were doing it. But if you didn't, it looked like we were abandoning the cause. When I explained that to him, that there was nothing nefarious going on, he was more annoyed than satisfied. He gave me a look, a look that said, "Don't you think we'd like to know that?"

He was right. We were so enamored with the system we had in place that we were missing the very people most impacted by the disaster. We had embarrassed him. We were soon able to adapt and find ways to embrace and absorb a more tactical situational awareness. It was a bit unique: we deployed Coast Guard cadets to each of the sixty-two local jurisdictions that bordered the Gulf waters, giving each local leader his or her own BLUF intelligence. They were no longer embarrassed, and we regained allies in an effort to protect their communities.

It may be misleading to consider the parish president's protests as noise at all. As much as it was important for the federal government to disclose what it knew to locals, we were destined to benefit from our response by opening up our lens to what they were capturing and seeing. We had been working in a vacuum we had created. Complainers were not cranks; they were completely accurate. In disaster management, there may very well be intelligence failures of epic proportions. As often as not, however, the failure also comes later. We haven't nurtured the capacity to absorb information, put it into digestible form, and relate it to those most likely impacted. Only by doing so can we hope to minimize the harms.

And we can do that now because the disaster could very well be, may very well be, tomorrow. The bells are always tolling. You are here.

CHAPTER THREE

UNITY OF EFFORT

*"The Craziest F***king Thing"*

It was just a routine software update, the kind the average person often ignores when it pops up on the screen. Overnight, if accepted, the software is somehow changed, allowing for upgrades or glitch fixes. In the spring of 2020, customers of the software technology company Solar-Winds were sent a software upgrade request. SolarWinds is a Texas-based company with powerful customers in government and the private sector. The upgrade was for its most popular product, called Orion. Orion is an internal management and detective system, which oversees a company's cyber capacity and organizes its assets and assesses any dramatic changes. SolarWinds clients received a message about Orion's upgrade and were told to type their password in and that the fixes would be made.

Bad start.

SolarWinds did not send an upgrade request. We now know that hackers, later identified by the United States government as the Russian intelligence service SVR, had infiltrated that system to insert malicious coding into Orion's software. Once in, that coding became the conduit for a major cyberattack against as many as eighteen thousand clients with precious and confidential assets. Companies like

Microsoft, Intel, and Cisco, in addition to federal agencies like the Departments of Justice, Energy, and Defense, all were victims. The Russians were essentially able to hide in America's systems for nearly nine months; they were spying, of course, and collecting information that SolarWinds' clients viewed as valuable. It was a "sophisticated adversary who took aim at a soft underbelly of digital life: the routine software update. The tradecraft was phenomenal," said Adam Meyers, who led the cyber forensics team hired by SolarWinds. The code was unique, somewhat simple and yet innovative. For Meyers, it was "the craziest f***ing thing I'd ever seen."[1]

The breach was not discovered by SolarWinds but by one of its clients, a well-known cybersecurity firm called FireEye. During its own security review, a FireEye security specialist happened to notice that one of the company's employees had registered two phones to access the network. The employee only knew of one. The second number was registered under his name but belonged to someone else. A monthlong internal investigation finally determined that it was the Orion upgrade request that had provided the opening.[2]

There is every inclination, and some of it understandable, to blame SolarWinds, though the nature of the breach—both so sophisticated and so basic—may have gone undetected by many companies. Solar-Winds publicized who its clients were, a not uncommon marketing tool but one that certainly gave adversaries the sense that they were a good, fruitful target. There were rumors about a password to one of the servers that was, no joke, "solarwinds123." (Don't do that!) And then there were former employees of SolarWinds who had left the company because they feared it was not taking security seriously enough. Whatever the reason, a mere system upgrade turned into one of the greatest cyber breaches of all time. Update available, the prompt said. In fact, the update unintentionally made a treasure trove of data available.

And the enemy walked right off with it.

GATES, GUARDS, AND GUNS

Unity of effort describes the planning we all can do to ensure a collectiveness when the boom arrives. Too often, preparedness is distributed, and security efforts are left vulnerable because the systems in place are too disjointed. The architecture of security is the idea that for an institution to maximize safety and security planning, it must first successfully establish a governance structure that embraces all players and capacities. Empowering the security apparatus will maximize capabilities when they are needed the most.

The security architecture must include just about every piece of the response capabilities. But in many companies and institutions, there is little attempt to unify and empower all these different silos, to create connective tissue around planning for consequence management. Responsibilities are often too divided internally; sometimes they are contracted out; licensees and clients are out of the chain of command; there is sometimes no management or board leadership directing it.

For so many institutions, safety is seen solely as some combination of the three Gs: gates, guards, and guns. It is always about purchases and gizmos and not about sustainable protocols. Companies move into headquarters, hire people, set up networks and systems, bolster supply chains and manufacturing, and connect people and goods all without thinking much about preparedness. When security does come up, they hire some folks who can do the job or consultants or freelance teams to fill in any blanks. This kind of planning is insufficient to handle recurrent challenges.

Just as a budget is a reflection of values—what you are willing to pay for—architecture is a reflection of priorities. For example, the US Forestry Service: it would be reasonable to think that it resides in the Department of the Interior, an agency intended to protect our animals; vegetation; and historic, tribal, and recreational lands. In fact,

THE DEVIL NEVER SLEEPS

the Forestry Service is in the Department of Agriculture. What does that say? It implies our government views our forests as a commodity rather than a natural preservation, much as it views cows or corn or soybeans. I focus on governance structures like this because I believe they signal the importance an institution has placed on preparedness and resilience. Place has meaning.

Security architecture can be very literal—not an abstract reflection of organizational design. The city of Oakland wanted to keep its professional baseball team, the Oakland A's, in the city. Major League Baseball was clamoring for a shinier stadium for the team, and the Oakland Athletics Investment Group, LLC, made its first choice for the site of the new stadium Howard Terminal, located in an industrial wasteland at the waterfront. The project anticipated games and concerts up to 103 days of the year along with other events throughout the year for an estimated total of 354 per year. Other elements of the proposed development included up to three thousand residential units, 1.5 million square feet of office space, up to 270,000 square feet of retail uses, and a four-hundred-room hotel.[3]

The project had tremendous support, but also significant detractors. The economic, social, and political debates notwithstanding, even a cursory review of the site exposed its problems.[4] Oakland experiences fires and earthquakes, mega events are targets for mass shootings, and even the most benign crowd can cause a massive stampede. Surrounded on one side by water, with just a few exit roads, some of which were consistently blocked by rail and cargo to keep the West Coast supply chain moving, there was no way that people could leave safely should something calamitous happen. That realization arrived, however, after a great deal had been invested in the site. An afterthought, it presented the team management with a serious challenge at a time when the battle lines were already drawn: build here and possibly die, or don't build here and risk the team going elsewhere. By the time the question of the security architecture was articulated, it was too late.

In the security world, the capacity of the safety apparatus to have a say in business planning is called *availability*. Is your team available when it matters the most? For many institutions, this question is answered with the most basic of analysis: yes, we know who to call. But availability is fundamentally about access: Are they available before you determine the location of the baseball field?

We all tend to focus on our core competencies, our mission. We don't see security as an enabler, but more as a nuisance or an add-on. That's a mistake. Instead, we must think about response capabilities as part of a core competency of the business and then figure out what features in that institution or community need the most protection. "It's not so much about the big bank, but about the things that the banks do," Chris Krebs, the former head of the Department of Homeland Security's Cyber and Infrastructure Security Agency, told me.[5]

Cash availability at a bank isn't really a big deal, remarked Krebs. "You'll find cash. But if the bank at JP Morgan, for instance, lost the ability to process wholesale payments (how employers pay their employees) on a daily basis . . . then we would have a global economic crisis."[6] This is a key point. A large financial institution's core value is in its distribution of large sums of money to employers who then distribute it to us. They are in the ATM business so that banking can be easy, but it isn't a necessity. Gates, guns, and guards can protect the ATM machines, but that isn't a big bank's compelling safety need. We risk greater damage if we don't figure out where the consequence management investments are needed to protect the most value.

Ask Colonial Pipeline. In May 2021, a ransomware attack on the Colonial Pipeline energy distribution company led to a dramatic but necessary response. They shut the entire system down. The cyberattackers, likely affiliated with the Russian government, didn't want much money; they set the ransom demand relatively low so that companies would be inclined to pay and not tell law enforcement. That's how ransomware works. Simply, everybody gets it over with; it's the price of doing business; the insurance industry even offers ransomware protection.

Colonial, however, is not a tech company. It is responsible for delivering gas and oil to nearly 45 percent of the Eastern Seaboard, a dependency that seems shocking for a critical infrastructure, but the distribution network was built up over time with little thought to diversification. When the attack was discovered, the company had no choice but to shut down the entire system. Not to do so would risk physical assets, including thousands of miles of piping. Colonial lost control of its network; it was worried that should it continue, it would be (in industry parlance) "pumping blind" with no transparency. Colonial later disclosed that it had, in fact, paid the ransom but that the cyberattackers proved unreliable in releasing their network even after the payment. So Colonial had to shut everything down.

How could Colonial Pipeline get hacked? It's a fair question, but the wrong one. A more significant question in our era of catastrophes is this: How, after so much investment in security planning, did Colonial have no tricks up its sleeve other than to shut down? That is not a

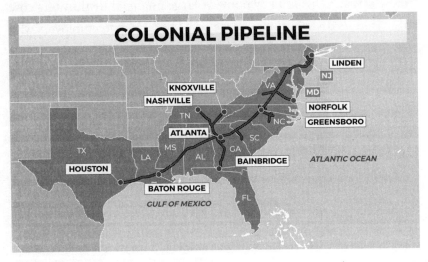

Scope of disruption when Colonial Pipeline shut down.

sustainable response. A day or two of closure was understandable. But longer? Imagine, instead, that Colonial had focused on the possibility that its core function would be disrupted. Yes, it would want to protect its networks better, but it might have thought through some, or any, disaster planning once the networks were breached. Maybe it shuts down immediately to determine the damage, but waiting another week is an unacceptable amount of time. It could have built backup, redundant networks that are deployed in such an event; separated key needs, such as those related to operations and distribution, from business ones, such as payroll on the network. It might have planned a recovery effort that focused on getting large pipelines moving quickly and relied on trucks and other forms of transportation for local delivery. A number of options were available if only the company had not separated cybersecurity from physical security. To call it an attack on a pipeline's cyber network is too benign; it was an attack on a pipeline. It was an attack on its value.

REARRANGING THE DECK CHAIRS

The old saying about the futility of rearranging deck chairs on the *Titanic* describes doing something pointless that is likely to be overtaken by larger events, such as hitting a massive iceberg and sinking. Focusing on design, this theory goes, distracts from the problem. Some of these "deck chair" arrangements can seem cosmetic in nature, but many are necessary to ensure that the structure can withstand a boom. Put more bluntly: to help minimize disruptions, it is important to look at the full picture. True, after a crisis or catastrophe, governments will often respond by doing some redecorating. They create new offices or bureaucracies, as if that one office or department would have stopped the damage. This sentiment was what compelled the creation of the Department of Homeland Security after the terror attacks on 9/11. More than two dozen offices and agencies from other departments were merged together into a massive behemoth whose capabilities and competencies have often been under scrutiny.

Many companies followed suit in our post-9/11 era, hiring a new legion of employees in the space, led by the newly minted chief security officer (CSO). The following decade, as companies were experiencing more and more cyberattacks, a new kind of leader rose: the chief information security officer (CISO). Even later, it turns out, as the country responded to the COVID-19 pandemic, some of these companies would hire a new type of officer, the chief medical officer (CMO) or chief health officer (CHO). That's a lot of C-people.

The sentiment was commendable in many instances, but the titles mean little without some cohesive tissue. The more important effort is whether all these different entities are aligned and unified. The CSO, often a former FBI or Secret Service agent, focuses mainly on things like badging, physical perimeter protection, and the whereabouts of VIPs. They hold trainings and exercises to make sure new and old employees are prepared for an active shooter or earthquake. The CISO, almost always a techie, is mostly focused on prevention efforts—to the left of the boom—securing the network from disruptions through password and layered defense controls. The new CMO or CHO, generally a public health expert, is now part of overall efforts

The many security roles in a C-suite.

to assess what bad germs or other evil viruses might be lurking out in the world that could impact the company or its supply chain. With divided efforts, focuses, and labor, they are often in different silos protecting companies from different risks. Hopefully, by this point, the problem is clear: when the ship goes down, the whole ship is going down.

Our tendency is to build bad architecture, to set the table as if everybody is only a party of one. Nowhere is this bad habit more obvious than in what has happened to the cybersecurity space in the last decade or so. We live in a world of physical threats, and that doesn't become less true even if we spend a lot of time online; the same is also true in reverse. The nexus between physical and cyber is a distinction without a difference; the enemy breaches a system, and that system will have an impact on what can be done, whether it is flying airplanes or delivering goods or pumping gas to the entire East Coast.

The division of responsibilities is often exacerbated by the lack of focus at the top. The different C-leaders in security not only have different reporting structures and chains of command, but they also rarely have a voice in leadership or on the board of directors. Few boards of directors for public companies have a single individual from the security or cybersecurity realm.[7] This is not merely a symbolic challenge; it says to the employees that their skills or expertise are not integral to the company's business model. It also denies those in security within the company any ability to access the top corporate leaders. Place matters—place at the table matters. Response capabilities are just not often viewed as business enablers.

This same attitude—"But we aren't in the security industry"—impacts a lot of the new economy as well. In Silicon Valley and the venture capitalist world, all the talk of security is a real drag. They like to think outside the box, disrupt, and change the world. A lot of them have built vast empires around those clichés. This includes the sharing economy: there it is blithely assumed that the platforms are all about connectivity and that bad things cannot happen. Their mottos essentially are about bringing people together: Uber, Lyft, WeWork, and Airbnb. The ability to build a community, with freedom and flexibility to boot, is their business model. Thinking about what crises that business model can lead to is not.

Bringing people together can create greater risk. This fact is neither good nor bad. But as the risks increased, the companies found themselves underprepared. Rideshares and shared living situations began to generate a lot of complaints about unsafe behavior by passengers, drivers, hosts, and guests. Some of those complaints became criminal investigations. By 2020, Uber had announced that there were no fewer than three thousand sexual harassment or sexual violence complaints against the company's drivers.[8] The company could not wish away the problem even if the status of the drivers—independent contractors—gave them some wishful plausible deniability. An Uber driver is an Uber driver regardless of his legal employment status.

Much of the Silicon Valley world, however, still did not give a place to the architects of safety. Many of the structures put into place were inconsistent with an integrated effort or transparency about what could happen. Advisory, or in the think-outside-the-box world of startups, "trust advisory," boards (because the word *trust* seems less scary than *security*) were established.[9] Fancy people, former cabinet secretaries, high-level folks who held special positions in government, gather around a table to discuss "trust." Trust: sounds nice, not intimidating, touchy-feely. That's the problem. Security architecture is serious stuff, and it can't be relegated to the equivalent of a kids' table at Thanksgiving.

Time and again, governance structures rather than lack of knowledge or capacity hinder our focus on response planning. We just think if we spend enough time on assessing risks, maybe some additional time on potential vulnerabilities, we have done enough. But we completely leave out rigorous consequence management, and often that is because so many don't view themselves as being in the security business. But we all are, whether we chose it or not. It might have been dumbfounding, but not shocking, that the Colonial Pipeline didn't have a disaster manager for cybersecurity breaches.

A unified effort will require looking for people and systems who have an eye toward the holistic nature of preparedness response and can drive company policies. A CEO, a small business owner, or anybody in charge of anything doesn't need to be an expert on planning or tactical operations but does have to allow for those systems to be fully nurtured at the company or institution. From the security team to board membership to vendors, every player is part of the disaster management team. Indeed, some of the greatest service disruptions did not happen because of a direct hit on a network but because the enemy entered through what we call a back door. SolarWinds was one such backdoor attack.

These unifying efforts can also seem overwhelming, especially for smaller business owners or entities that can barely buy a lock for the door. It need not be. Earlier, I wrote of an all-hazards approach to consequence management. Basically, I asked that we suspend any notion that we need to prejudge what form the devil will actually take. Our focus should be on minimizing the consequences of his arrival. The standard of success is whether our reaction results in some metric called *less bad*. This notion of shared risks can be applied to shared responses. The best way to do this is to focus on dual-use capabilities.[10] The term *dual use* comes from the world of international relations and export controls. It refers to any technology that might be used for both peaceful and military aims, like a satellite or thermal imaging. Those items are generally under greater security review in their manufacturing and distribution. Dual use began to be applied widely to the world of response and preparedness a few years after the terror attacks on 9/11.

In the immediate aftermath of that day, and in the years that followed, tremendous resources were spent to buy local, state, and federal responders lots of, for want of a better word, gizmos. These were specialized devices so unique, like bioterror masks, that they were unlikely to be used. It was not sustainable. Eventually, response agencies began to understand that those purchases and items that could be used for many purposes were the most valuable. It can be as simple as a high-powered hose. Firefighters don't need a special hose for terror threats, another for arson, a third for natural fires. A hose will do. The benefit of the good old-fashioned hose was that it would be used frequently enough that responders would be familiar with it to use regardless of the situation.

We need to think of our preparedness architecture in a similar vein, unifying rather than bifurcating or specializing. These divisions were highlighted again as COVID-19 began to impact industries in the United States. During the pandemic, I found myself on the phone with the leadership of a major US retailer with thousands of brick-and-mortar stores throughout the US. I did not know that the CEO and his team were on the line yet and in my usual way was riffing with my team as if we were alone (this was right before we all turned to Zoom). "I guess it is up to me to tell them they are closing every facility?" I said with typical gallows humor.

"That can't be," a voice on the other end of the line chimed. It was the CEO.

After a half hour of explaining the likely consequences of COVID-19, it finally became clear to him. It wasn't that I was particularly prescient or wise, disclosing some hidden truth that the CEO was reluctant to hear. What was amazing about it was that he hadn't heard the possibility of an all-store closure before. It was never in the company's plans. How could that possibly be? From what I could tell, tens of millions of dollars had been spent on security efforts for the company, but those were focused on gates, guards, and guns. A potential new threat, whose likelihood may have been low but its consequences high, never factored into the planning of this *Fortune* 100 company. Its board of directors, filled with other CEOs and their friends, as is often the case, didn't have the breadth of expertise to force the company to look at what was unfolding.

There is a common refrain among first responders that you don't want to be handing out business cards at the scene of destruction. It is a little old school (we don't do business cards anymore). But every leader now has a capacity to ensure that the architecture of their institution is aligned for unity of effort. You don't want the physical security gal to be meeting the cyber response guy at the moment of impact.

THE WOMAN CHECKING LUGGAGE

Peter Neffenger, former head of the Transportation Security Administration (TSA), didn't know who the woman with three stripes on her uniform was. Neffenger had inherited an agency so fundamentally broken—it was the summer of 2015, immediately following publicly leaked reports that TSA had spectacularly failed a number of internal covert screening tests, and TSA was in a crisis—that nothing short of a direct call from the president convinced him to take the job. Over the remainder of that year, TSA experienced an epic breakdown that wasn't entirely under its control, causing massive lines and dismayed passengers in airports across the country. More people were flying, and fewer people than anticipated had applied for Pre-Check programs. TSA had too many unfilled positions, and as airlines started to charge for checked items, more people were trying to bring more things through security checkpoints.[11] As Neffenger took over, he had a problem. The security agents who checked luggage, who were the frontline to get passengers from one side to the other, felt alienated from an agency whose very name has the word *security* in it. And he had just learned why.

The woman wore three stripes, the number to designate a frontline security supervisor. She oversaw the security checkpoint of a major airport, where TSA became the retail face of government as millions of travelers passed through daily. Neffenger had decided he needed to be on the ground to discover how the proverbial "ship had been built." The woman stared at her new boss with daggers in her eyes. Neffenger told me that he had met her during his nomination process, before he was officially confirmed: "She looked at me and she said, 'You know you're like every other guy in a suit that walks in this room, you come in here, you give us all this happy talk about how you care for us and take care of us and you're the first guy to write my name on a bus and drive over me when something bad happens.'"[12]

She had some thoughts, serious, helpful ones. She was at the front of the organization, in charge of protecting air travel, yet she had no sense of identity or unity with the nonpublic side of the organization. She saw them as the bus, ready to drive over her. That disconnect made any sense of unity of effort impossible. She seemed to know she had her moment; she asked Neffenger to come work with her for a few days one week. He arrived, the head of the organization, like a scene from the TV show *Undercover Boss*. She told him that most trainees wore white shirts and black pants when they arrived, but she excused his khakis. Neffenger spent days there with the woman with the three stripes. He wore the correct uniform by Tuesday. Neffenger, a naturally talkative person, found himself easily chatting with passengers, asking them how they were or where they were heading. He loved it.

But the woman had other ideas. "You can't talk to people; you're gonna get in trouble with the TSA."

"But I am TSA," Neffenger replied.

The sentiment, however, was based on the reality that security agents were trained to believe every passenger was a potential terrorist, so the last thing you want is to engage them. TSA leadership understood, however, that it was being judged by other metrics:

counterterrorism, certainly, but also flow, friendliness, and customer engagement. But the security front, the actual TSA agents in the airports, had never been trained for that. TSA had actually established a rule that too much engagement—too much interaction—meant that a line worker's pay could be docked. It was a miserable experience for everyone involved.

The changes that Neffenger put into place were fundamentally structural ones to create more unity of effort. The woman with three stripes was brought into the front office to help Neffenger better understand what training and rules were needed for the frontline that made it a safe and secure effort, but one that also understood that friendliness and engagement were likely to make the experience for the public better. He linked security with business operations. He aligned the front team with the back team. She, and the teams she represented, had a seat at the table. Changes were made in the entire security apparatus, from hiring to training. And, most importantly, Neffenger made clear that should this experiment go awry, the bus should be directed at him.

The process of unification can start now. Take a piece of paper and consider the problem: If X, Y, or Z were to happen, is there a centralized system of response wherever you sit? Trying to map it out will be a helpful exercise; gaps and duplications will be exposed. Who is at the table? Where do they sit? Design drives a culture; value is set at the top. Unity of effort is foundational, but first it must be built.

The devil is willing to throw any of us under the bus. We can begin to design better for that now. You are here.

CHAPTER FOUR

AVOID THE LAST LINE OF DEFENSE TRAP

A Very Big, Broken Vacuum Cleaner

They said it would work. All of the energy companies who perform offshore drilling said it would absolutely, positively work. No problem, they told regulators and legislators: if anything ever went wrong on the ocean floor (and surely it would—this is offshore drilling, after all) as oil under the seabed was captured, the single blowout preventer (BOP) would take charge, automatically shutting down the system to protect the oceans from any spill damage. They said it would work.

It didn't.

The rest, as they say, is history. In early 2010, an oil-drilling rig named *Deepwater Horizon* was deployed in the Macondo Prospect area in the Gulf of Mexico. On April 20, 2010, the rig exploded due to unregulated pressure from the oil capture that eventually could not be contained. The rig sank, killing eleven workers. The backup plan—the BOP—then failed, leading to the largest oil spill in US history across vast swaths of the coast and surface of the Gulf. "We have a game changer," Captain Mary Landry told the anxious Obama administration team on a call a few days after the explosion. The oil, she told them, could not be contained.[1] "Game changer" would turn out to be an understatement. Oil spilled through the waters of the Gulf states, from Texas to the marshlands of Louisiana, across the beaches of Mississippi and Alabama, and straight across the panhandle of Florida. Most of the ocean would be closed to fishing, impacting a food supply chain delivering fish throughout the United States. Summer tourism would come to a standstill.

Imagine an average vacuum cleaner. It is plugged in, and it captures the dust and dirt from the carpet. It is a pretty perfect invention. If the bag should break, you turn the cleaner off so that the dirt doesn't spill everywhere. But suppose the bag breaks and the machine won't turn off, and even the final safety feature of unplugging the cleaner fails? The vacuum relentlessly sucks up dirt and dust, the bag ruptures, and the dust and debris are blown all over the room in a growing cloud of mess. That's what happened to create the biggest oil spill in history: the vacuum cleaner's bag was ripped, and unplugging the device failed.

The consequence was historic. By the end, 4.9 million barrels of oil was discharged; 48,200 responders were engaged in oil spill response; 9,700 vessels were deployed to try to clean up the oil before it got to shore; eighteen million gallons of dispersants were released into ocean or air to try to break up the oil; 127 surveillance aircraft monitored the mess from above.[2] Oil was everywhere. I saw where the rig went down on a flyover with the governor of Louisiana, Bobby Jindal: the Coast Guard had deployed some boats, and they were like little sand dots against waves and waves of oil.[3]

The BP oil spill was a political, environmental, economic, and historic crisis. Oil drilling over the years had gotten more aggressive, extending out into the oceans in hopes of capturing more oil. The company didn't even know how big the Macondo Prospect area of the Gulf of Mexico was. For all any of us knew, the well could spill for years. Of the five Republican governors running states impacted by the spill, three—Louisiana's Bobby Jindal, Texas's Rick Perry, and Mississippi's Haley Barbour—would eventually seek to replace President Obama in the 2012 election for his second term. Offshore big oil, an industry not aligned with the green economy of the future, was put at risk. In light of the spill, the Obama administration also put a moratorium on all offshore drilling throughout the entire nation. With a dirty ocean and a moratorium, the entire Gulf was frozen: no fishing, no drilling, no tourism.

They said it would work.

FAILURE MODE

The first chapters focused on structural and strategic investments that can be made now, because tomorrow is too late to prepare for when the devil comes again. They highlight how we are sitting on the verge of the boom, always, and they examine the need to assume breach, capture the noise, and build unified response mechanisms that would help anyone be ready for the inevitable. All are necessary, but any will do. The more each of us can take ownership of the inevitable boom, the less damage will ensue. The next chapters focus on the best practices that should be made, or avoided, before the boom strikes to give more opportunity to limit the losses that might otherwise occur. These, too, can be done now because tomorrow is too late.

Every disaster is going to look in retrospect like there was a moment when it could no longer be contained, when the right side of the boom was breached. It is called the single point of failure, and it describes the mechanism that causes the whole system to falter when it goes down. The BOP was, after all, that last line of defense. When it failed, the mess was uncontainable. The last line of defense is, ultimately, a crutch. The moment you find it, you are in trouble. That is because it reinforces a binary notion of preparedness: either the boom happened (the last line of defense worked), or it didn't (the last line of defense failed). The last line of defense is a trap and is conceptually harmful for three important reasons.

It can, first, provide a false sense that all is well if the last line of defense is not breached. But when a disaster happens, we often think, "What did we miss?" in the singular. Systems go down for all sorts of reasons, and if we think there is only one reason, then there is a tendency to neglect all the other reasons and ignore what could be done to minimize the impact should any one or all of them falter. In a world where we must focus on consequence minimization, protecting the single point of failure is the bare minimum; other failures may exist, and cumulatively they can result in the same harms that a single failure would cause.

Engineers often seek to counter this wishful thinking that surrounds so much of our planning by utilizing failure mode analysis. The more formal name is FMEA, failure mode and effects analysis, though it is often just called failure modes, and the plural actually seems more apt. It describes the process of assessing, testing, and reviewing the systems and subsystems, assembly lines, and components to identify beforehand the potential failures and then, ultimately, their effects. The FMEA is a very formal system; engineers use worksheets and qualitative scoring, mathematical rates, and statistical failure ratios in a very structured technique.

Essentially, the process—originating in the 1950s—is used at numerous points in the product life cycle of a new invention. The FMEA tries to figure out a potential failure of the invention and tests its reliability.[4] The process is part of a larger system of checks known as the Six Sigma tools.[5] These are assessment tools that are used to improve business efforts and productivity. Besides the FMEA, they include control charts and system checks. It is a highly technical effort, but the overall goal is to provide real-time analysis before too much is invested in a system that is doomed to fail. There are other names organizations often use to stress test preparedness, such as a systems dynamic review, scenario planning, or the mouthful hazard analysis and critical control point.[6] The latter was originally designed for food safety and supply-chain protection to better identify and evaluate potential hazards entering our bodies. It was so rigorous with its focus on testing "critical control points" of the food chain that it is now utilized in other fields.[7] These processes also have a secondary benefit: they force us to adapt in a culture of continuous improvement.

Even companies not in the engineering business can fail. Total reliance on the idea of avoiding a single point of failure tends to focus our attention on just one solution and helps us neglect the larger and systemic weaknesses that can lead to the disaster. The *Deepwater Horizon* rig had what they believed was a perfectly suitable BOP, but they had no fail-safe for when the fail-safe failed. A single safety feature cannot match a system analysis of what the effects of any failures will be and how to mitigate them. *Less bad* is the standard we are always aiming for here. A single last line of defense keeps institutions from thinking about how multiple lines of defense can help minimize the damage that is surely going to come.

A second reason for avoiding total reliance on the last line of defense planning is that it puts a lot of pressure on that single defense. The BOP is a significant investment in safety planning; it is not accurate to claim there are no safety features in offshore drilling. "Anyone who wants to be well-versed in oil drilling must understand the crucial role of the blowout preventer (BOP)," reads one internal safety document.[8] Its role was well known: "Essentially, a blowout preventer (BOP) shuts off the valve leading underneath the machinery to stop any liquid from surfacing in a dangerous explosion, or a kick," a blog post for the website of Keystone Energy Tools announces, as it offers new and used ones for sale.[9] But the word *essentially* is doing a lot of work here. BP's BOP weighed four hundred tons and was nearly five stories high. It was a monstrosity by itself. As it monitored the seafloor, it was designed with hydraulically powered devices that would simply (the word *simply* never did so much work) cut the oil that passed through it and then seal the well—or turn the vacuum off.

When BP's BOP most needed to work, it didn't. An explosion, oil and gas everywhere, a rig on fire, a surprised crew under the debris now spewing from the well, landing on their heads—this was the BOP's moment. After all, BOPs are not designed carelessly. Critics of the industry are quick to dismiss the efforts in safety and security made by these companies. They may not commit to safety because their hearts are in the right place, certainly. Business and industry continuity matter most. Whatever the motivation, a 2011 study by the UC Berkeley–based Center for Catastrophic Risk Management found that BP's BOP had at least six redundant—in other words, additional—means to activate. That is smart design. But every single one of those systems failed, and $65.8 billion in damage followed.[10]

The BOP's failures were not singular in nature. This last line of defense had multiple vulnerabilities. Upon review, numerous studies found significant and fundamental flaws in the design of *all* BOPs. A 2012 study by the National Academies found that a "blind shear ram," a component meant to cut and seal pipe, "was not designed to shear all types and sizes of pipe that might be present."[11] A later 2014 study by the US Chemical Safety and Hazard Investigation Board, which investigates industrial accidents, noted that BOPs often become unworkable if any part of the piping it was designed to cut off is either buckled or twisted.[12] If the BOP is needed, it is likely to be needed during a catastrophic event in which the piping is in some disarray and under stress. Yet that is when it was found unlikely to work.

The Program on Government Oversight put it succinctly: "Bolts mysteriously break. Seals leak. Components get clogged. Torrents of gas and sand rip through steel. Design defects surface years after devices are put to work. Inspectors allegedly cut corners on inspections. Energy companies falsify safety tests. Operating instructions that leave little margin for error collide with messy and overwhelming forces."[13] The government has some responsibility for this. It "conceded and halved the mandated frequency of tests" and never updated rules despite all the studies that told them that they should. In May 2012, at a forum the Bureau of Safety and Environmental Enforcement held on blowout preventers, the National Academy of Engineering's McCarthy made a basic observation: "If these things are going to be expected to work under conditions where all hell is breaking loose, they have to be tested in conditions that simulate all hell breaking loose."[14]

Because sooner or later, hell always breaks loose.

This leads to the third, and most consequential, reason for rejecting the last line of defense planning. It can make us assume that, once breached, that failure is a steady state. And this was true for BP. Once the BOP was compromised, they had nothing they could do to manage the catastrophic situation and minimize the disruption. They had no defense after their last line had failed.

The BP industrial disaster began on April 20, 2010, when the BP-operated *Deepwater Horizon* exploded and the BOP failed. Oil spilled until the company could effectively close the well. That proved to be a problem because they had not trained or planned for this contingency: How do you close a well a mile under the ocean? On September 3, the three-hundred-ton failed blowout preventer was removed from the well and a replacement blowout preventer was installed. The well was called "effectively dead" on September 19.

Between April and September, BP unsuccessfully tried to close the well using every device and technique imaginable: drilling fluids, cement "top kill," a containment dome. BP achieved only a little relief on July 15 when a device finally was able to stop the flow, but it was a temporary measure and not terribly secure. It was over two months later that the well was finally declared dead. Late-night comics and social media had a lot of fun mocking BP's very public attempts to close the well. Neither BP, nor the industry, nor the government that sought to help had any plan for when the last line of defense faltered.

The independent congressional commission of the BP spill found that the industry had, for far too long, told regulators that the BOP was reliable, that it could survive the pressure of a blowout, and it began to believe it.[15] They said it would work, and so they didn't plan for when it didn't. They believed in the mythology that a last line of defense was some form of guarantee rather than a blind hope. A *less bad* strategy was never nurtured; there was nothing to the right of the boom except watching the ocean floor spew oil for months.

THEY SAID IT WAS BEAUTIFUL

The way any complicated system of safety works is that it first envisions layers of security, addressing not a single point of failure but multiple points of failure. For left-of-boom prevention planning, the hope is that you make it harder for the devil to reach his destination: the more barriers, the better. It sounds tricky, but it is conceptually easy to understand. We try to create a maze of obstacles and barriers so that the path to destruction becomes that much harder. A delayed boom is a success. But the boom will come. We need to begin to think about successive responses for the right side of the boom. Should the last line of defense fail, we need to create layered responses that could limit the impact.

Paradise, California, was appropriately named. It was once just that. Now, we can't think of the small town north of Sacramento without recalling the massive fire that swept through it on November 8, 2018, killing eighty-five of its residents, many of them in their cars on a single-lane road that leads to Paradise's ridge. At its peak, the fire was burning the equivalent of eighty football fields a minute. It destroyed eighteen thousand structures, fourteen thousand of them homes, and burned an area approximately the size of Chicago.[16]

Paradise was not just beautiful; it was an experiment. Its growth was part of a national movement known as the WUI, the wildland-urban interface. The WUI was the fastest-growing land use type in the US between 1990 and 2010. In the US, the migration of retiring baby boomers as they sought smaller communities and lower costs of living, with scenic and recreational resources, contributed to its growth. Climate change also drove these population shifts as people moved away from angrier oceans and eroding coasts. The WUI is where residential and commercial areas meet—even intermingle—in forests prone to wildfires.[17]

As people moved to developments like Paradise, their preferences for how to live clashed with how nature intended things to be. And the design of Paradise was indifferent to nature—it seemed to assume that nature would adapt to the incomers' landscaping preferences. Those included keeping the forest and trees as lush as possible. To make Paradise a paradise, planners avoided the very things that people were happy to leave behind: wide highways, multilane streets, traffic. The route to Paradise, then, was mostly through a single road appropriately called Skyway, which traversed the mountain ridge up to the town. It was unwelcoming to all but those who lived there, and that was the point.

I visited Paradise after the fire. The town was traumatized, and a majority of its residents were not likely to return. Insurance had been paid out, and many took their checks and moved. But something else amazing was happening: Paradise was preparing for the next fire and all the ones after that. And although Paradise has been spared over the last several years, wildfires have burned through other WUI communities. It is not surprising. The earth is warmer, the soil dryer, and the fires deadlier. There's no point in denying it; just do what you can to get ready.

There were three key areas that helped the community reimagine what it might do should there be a failure of a last line of defense, mainly containment of the fire. It sounds odd, but communities are learning to live through fire. The first is simple: design homes in a way that respects the land, and create different zones around a house that could absorb a fire. Fireproof materials, well-watered plants, and areas cleared of debris could mean that a resident could stay inside safely in the event of a fire.

Calli-Jane DeAnda, the executive director at the Butte County Fire Safe Council in Paradise, walked me through the thinking: keep the flammables away from the structure and give the fire food but no access to people. "As far as the (house) yard goes, what we're looking at is a really clean space, first five feet from the structure," in terms of vegetation, she said. "And the most critical part is that [the plants] are well watered." Watered plants are healthier and less combustible, and they therefore slow the speed of any fire.[18]

The second area was access. The ridge road runs two thousand feet above sea level. It is stunning, but deadly. There would have been no rational reason to build a road there except to let people live in isolation. Most of the streets in Paradise are dead ends lest someone drive over a cliff. The evacuation routes are limited; their design limitations were fatal during the first fire. But there are ways to fix that as well. Designers are laying down more asphalt so it can absorb heat better, making it harder for tires to melt, for cars to be stranded and engulfed. Wider clearings along the key roads mean that first responder personnel can travel more easily and broken-down cars can be moved aside without hindering access roads.

But the third and most important feature has to do with the fire itself. The Paradise fire started when the winds increased and a power line twenty miles from the town fell. There is a lot to say about our critical infrastructure and the need to keep it updated and safe to prevent such fires, but for the sake of argument—and the themes of this book—let's assume that's not an option for today. Once started, the fire took a path that wasn't necessarily preordained. Paradise was built in a way that let the fire kill.[19]

Over the years of WUI, the forest around Paradise had become a tinderbox. There were too many trees, too much brush. The unintended but totally foreseeable consequences of the WUI is that it interrupted the natural cycle of smaller, less devastating fires. Nature intended fire; without smaller fires, too much kindling for the flames accumulated. As a result, the underbrush that naturally would have been removed by fire grew unnaturally dense, and a fire that otherwise would have run out of fuel became a megafire. So for people to live in the WUI, they would need for nature to live as intended: accepting occasional small fires to avoid the bigger ones.

Forest Fire Consequence Minimization:
(a.k.a. How to Save a Life)

1. Home Design

2. Evacuation Routes

3. Deforestation

Forests are not supposed to be dense; fires can be slowed and minimized, buying time so that residents are not stuck relying on a potential single point of failure on their way out. One way to visualize it is that forests are supposed to be spaced out enough in a way that you can imagine a horse riding through the trees. "We're just trying to help show them that in order to slow the progress of the fire itself, this is what you need to do," Trevor McAntry, who coordinates tree removal for the town, told me. In a plaid shirt and a beard down to his chest, he stood there with his team, chainsawing perfectly healthy trees. "You need to be able to ride that horse."[20] It may not be pretty, but thinning—when planners purposely rid forests of trees by sawing them down or burning them—works. It deprives the fire of what is called the *fuel ladder*, easily accessible trees that burn fast.

These efforts, cumulatively, are necessary for the WUI experiment to work. They do not presuppose an impenetrable last line of defense, but rather multiple responses when it fails. Like layered defenses, layered responses will save lives and limit damage. The plan must assume that the last line of defense will fail and the fire will come.

We need to avoid single points of failure because they tend to fail. Engineers may talk in fancy terms like *sigmas* and *FMEAs*, but a civilian can perform due diligence. First, and obviously, assess the single point of failure and create another and maybe even a few more. The cockpit door can't be the only protection for pilots. The offshore oil industry fought against backup blowout preventers as a condition of drilling. True, blowout preventers don't always work, but you increase your chances a lot by having more than one. This is what dual authentication for our iPhones does. Two entry points are better than one.

And then make sure that simple point is protected. We already do this for some industries: hospitals have separate generator systems to keep the electricity flowing so that they are not dependent, in the middle of an operation, on benign weather. Many people buy generators at home for the same reason. The backup doesn't need to replicate the whole system—we don't need to build two hospitals—but to be enough to cover and protect the core needs.

Layered defenses should also be separated so they aren't impacted by each other's failures. Airplanes, again, provide a good example because the consequences of a crash tend to be binary: alive or dead. On July 19, 1989, United Airlines Flight 232, a McDonnell Douglas DC 10, crashed at Sioux City, Iowa, after what is called an "uncontained engine failure" earlier in the flight mistakenly disabled all hydraulic systems and made all flight controls completely inoperable. In a fortunate twist of fate, on board was a DC-10 flight instructor, and also a deadhead, who was able to perform a partially controlled emergency landing by steering the remaining two engines. One hundred eighty-five people on board survived, but 111 others died, and the plane was completely destroyed.[21]

There were two hydraulic fuses, so what the heck happened? The designers of what is often described as a horribly flawed airplane actually were quite smart in addressing a potential single point of failure: just one hydraulic system. So they put in a second. Smart. Except they fed the additional hydraulic tubes through a narrow setting, side by side, under the tail engine, so when the engine failed, so did the hydraulic fuses. Due to their close proximity under the tail engine, the engine failure ruptured the backup contingency as well. And the resulting losses—to the rudder, flaps, elevators, spoilers, horizontal stabilizers, everything—led to the loss of life.[22]

NO REGRETS AND AN EXIT

The process of planning around the last line of defense will likely illuminate ways in which preparedness and response planning can be better managed for the future when the devil comes again. Engineers I have worked with call it a "no regrets" improvement. Maybe what you find in a review won't actually be that consequential if fixed, but what's the harm? If not needed this time, the devil is sure to return again. This effort keeps institutions constantly moving, assessing, managing around potential impacts. They don't become static: What's the harm— no regrets—of tidying this or that up a bit?

This process will also expose whether it isn't worth rethinking the whole plan. Engineers do it all the time. If the design is fundamentally flawed, start all over. If the devil is coming again and again, no amount of tinkering is going to fix a fundamentally flawed system. A last line of defense review could disclose that the entire system needs a do-over. We shouldn't be afraid of this possibility. Since disasters are no longer random or rare, at some stage that determination will have to be made. Better to make it now before the next disaster arrives.

Today, it is still fair to ask whether the only solution to climate change and recurring fires is to abandon places where we now live. The

WUI is a good example. Fires are larger and more frequent; of the ten most destructive forest fires in California, six occurred in the thirteen months prior to Paradise. The climate changes mean there is more rain than there used to be in winter, creating a different kind of fuel for growth of plants and forestry in the winter months. That dense forest then dries out in the summer with the heat and lack of rain. The winds then come, and all it takes is a single spark.

We need to accept when a system's points of failure are ultimately so vulnerable that we should no longer move forward. There is risk in everything we do, and we will be judged if we dismiss it rather than manage it. But at some stage, the risks may become too great, too difficult to manage. That is when retreat may be the ultimate consequence minimization technique. Any realistic assessment of potential damage has to recognize the point where losses are no longer acceptable. Take Paradise's options, for example. Yes, they could build differently, design roads differently, let the forests grow differently, but ultimately, are those modifications enough to face down climate change and the pace and heat of new fires?

About Paradise, there are already people who say the risk of rebuilding is too great. "We are at a stage where we shouldn't rebuild," Jesse Keenan, a design professor at Tulane University, concluded. "We shouldn't be putting future people and kids at risk. And that may mean 'managed retreat,' where you guide people as they transition from one place to another, from a high risk to a place where they can manage the risk better."[23]

"Managed retreat" is anything but gentle and is often called planned relocation.[24] Any exercise in assessing potential single points of failure in response to a boom has to leave retreat as an option. It is a movement that is gaining traction across the globe, and surprisingly the US has been doing it for decades, but often too late. After a disaster, many local governments will allow homeowners to assess their predisaster value and move, with the government willing to provide up to 75 percent of the homeowner's home value. Not all homeowners can do this: the government will determine the likelihood that the building will be damaged again (in a world where disasters were seen as flukes, this made sense). In the twenty years before 2017, FEMA reported forty-three thousand voluntary buyouts across the US and territories.[25] President Biden's infrastructure bill, passed in late 2021, may be the first major piece of US legislation that accepts climate change as a given. It provides funding for stronger buildings, disaster adaptations, and even managed retreats.[26] Biden appointed Mitch Landrieu, the former mayor of New Orleans—a city accustomed to climate disasters—to oversee the distribution of funds. This is a tremendous shift because the changes are not waiting for the next disaster to happen. If we assume more and more disasters will come, then a managed retreat before the next disaster occurs needs to be a realistic response to planning. Sometimes there are no more last lines of defense.

One of the challenges of focusing on consequence minimization is that the long-term, durable solutions—focus on climate change, buttress global health efforts—are daunting. But until that time comes, much damage can be minimized. The devil will come, and the best we can do is anticipate his arrival. Every institution has the capacity to assess its single points of failure, to assume the last line of defense is not that, and then focus on avoiding losses that are not inevitable.

Less bad is our standard. You are here.

CHAPTER FIVE

STOP THE BLEED

Combat Reality

As the US entered the wars in Afghanistan and Iraq in the 2000s, it sent its military trained with dated practices. Standard operating procedure was to get a bleeding soldier to medical help as soon as practicable. In traditional wars, that would mean carrying a hurt soldier away from enemy lines to a medic tent or back to base. But homemade bombs and improvised explosive devices (IEDs) in urban arenas made the nature of warfare different. There were no dedicated battle zones. The military had not changed its rules of engagement in response to a new warfare; it had not changed its battlefield medicine.

The military did try to prevent the new kind of injuries it encountered. Specifically, it designed novel vehicles that could withstand IED (usually roadside bombs, occasionally suicide vehicles) attacks, such as the Mine-Resistant Ambush Protected (MRAP) light tactical vehicle. From 2007 to 2012 alone, twelve thousand of these new vehicles were manufactured and deployed. Combat troops also had new body armor design and materials, the thought being that with lightweight but durable gear, soldiers would not be injured should they be in proximity to the explosive device. Both efforts served to protect soldiers. But if those prevention efforts failed, and they often did, the practice was to move injured soldiers to a medical facility, however far away it might be.

Close to 70 percent of injuries of US soldiers during the wars were due to improvised bombs.[1] These injuries, if not immediately treated, could result in a soldier bleeding out. The consequence was death. So a radical change in the military was needed to help save these men and women once they had already suffered a grave injury.[2] The Pentagon had to devise new ways to treat soldiers—once harmed—in a different way. The military began to adopt a "stop the bleed" effort. A wounded soldier, after all, is not necessarily a dead soldier.

This may seem obvious to us, but there were reasons why it took a while for the stop the bleed program to be fully adopted. Urban warfare is dangerous, and medical assistance provided on the spot left soldiers vulnerable to more attacks. Another reason was the persistent, though erroneous, belief that the best way to stop the bleed—tying a tourniquet near the wound to compress circulation and stop the flow of blood from an artery or a vein—might instead lead to an amputation or death if fitted too tightly.

Clearly, the survival of a soldier was much more important than any fears of amputation.[3] So instead of waiting to medically evacuate a soldier to hospital care, the military changed its procedures to train other field soldiers, mostly nonmedics, to help their team should one suffer after an attack. This was key: it was a way to minimize the harm after the bleeding had already begun. These changes in protocol were focused on the obvious truth that massive bleeding was the most urgent need. "You've got four minutes to get someone oxygen so their brain doesn't start to die. But you really only have a few pumps of the heart before they've lost so much blood they're not going to be able to live," Colonel Patricia Hastings, a doctor, told Medical Xpress.[4]

Stop the bleed. And fast. The new protocols were adopted because the military recognized that the environment it was working in was different from any other it had worked in before. Doctors and researchers determined that the Pentagon's training was influenced too much by civilian emergency medicine—say, a car accident—and not enough by modern-day combat reality.

This effort was then buttressed with changes to tourniquet technology and materials—including blood-clotting medicines soldiers carried—that assisted to stop the bleed. These clotting agents, combined with new tourniquet-like devices that were designed for the areas of a body most likely to be impacted, have been successful. For large injuries, new foams have been created that can be injected into a large wounded cavity, creating pressure to stop the bleed and buying some time until medical assistance is available. Where body parts are exposed, such as the shoulder or groin, new injections of little sponges are administered by syringe that will absorb the blood, like a gauze. All of these worked. When the Pentagon reviewed tourniquet use in 862 cases in Iraq, nearly 90 percent of the soldiers survived. None of them required amputation.

Stop the bleed after the bleeding has begun.

CASCADING LOSSES

The tourniquet example is an ideal one for understanding an imperative in recurring-disaster management: stop the bleed, or *minimize cascading losses*, in crisis management jargon. Essentially, the strategy doesn't assume that all disasters are an on/off switch between nothing happening (left-of-boom efforts were successful) and everything happening (the damage is catastrophic). In the previous chapter, I urged against overreliance on the notion of a last line of defense. The idea that there is one thing that, if working properly, could stop the tragedy is a crutch that undermines creative planning and preparation for systems that will get hit by disasters time and time again.

Cascading losses describe the phenomenon when the disaster's impacts flow and accumulate, exponentially increasing the harm. To minimize such disruptions, systems must be built that recognize that some harm may already have occurred—the soldier has been hit by an IED—but more harm may follow. Imagine the BP scenario differently, then, if BP had put less faith in their last line of defense; imagine a ten-day spill, not one that lasts more than one hundred days. The most obvious investment would have been a second on-hand BOP. It would have been expensive, but not $68 billion expensive. It could have served as a backup possibly; it might have prevented some, though not all, of the spill. The company might have also tested the capacity to close a well so far down under the water; it might have tried these techniques with different water pressures and temperatures; it might have tested underwater dispersants that could break the oil up or surface ones that could help it evaporate under a Gulf sun; it might have tested new techniques for burning oil, collecting oil, or keeping it offshore. It might have been compelled by the government to do all of the above. But neither self-interest nor government regulations moved the company.

Managing how we can slow cascading losses forces us out of the binary box of disaster management and focuses on how we might better fail safely. There is a term to describe technology like this: a fail-safe. A fail-safe feature is a specific design that is created to keep a device safe in the event of a total systemic meltdown. It is not designed to prevent failure but to mitigate the consequences should a failure come to pass when the last line of defense falters. Engineers and designers are often trained to create a fail-safe, knowing that to design something that never fails is admirable but very unlikely.

We've come to depend on fail-safe design in our lives even if we don't know it. At amusement parks, our kids pay money to voluntarily sit on swings, attached by chain links, to a central hub that then elevates them and circles round and round. They look dangerous, but a sophisticated design (one hopes!) will have a safe-to-fail feature so that should there be an emergency, the swings will descend, carefully, to the ground level rather than remain up high. This will make any evacuation easier, even though some kids may like the thrill of remaining suspended in air.[5]

A fail-safe that limits cascading losses serves as a good analogy for disaster management planning in a world where disasters keep coming. What do you wish you had in place to stop the bleed? From large to small businesses, at home or out in the world, minimizing cascading losses is not a huge investment. It merely requires us to figure out the best proverbial tourniquets. It need not be one device or instrument but a series of investments, procedures, and training that are based on the irrefutable assumption that something will fail and that our goal is to help them fail more safely.

"FRANK, WE LOST THE A FEED"[6]

New Orleans was set to host the XLVII Super Bowl on February 3, 2013. The Baltimore Ravens and the San Francisco 49ers were pitted against each other. Two brothers, John and Jim, coached each team. The game was dubbed for their shared last name, the "Harbaugh Bowl." The event, at the city Superdome, was also being billed as a public celebration for the city and arena, both devastated by Hurricane Katrina in 2005. Many in New Orleans had rushed to the Superdome during the flooding, but officials were not prepared for their arrival. The stadium itself was damaged; the electricity did not flow. Images of the dead, some laid out on chairs and covered in sheets outside the flooded Superdome, were haunting.

About eighteen months before the game, Entergy New Orleans, which supplies electricity to the Superdome, replaced devices known as switchgears. Switchgears managed energy levels and fed into two cables—the A and B feed—that are buried underground. Those cables end at the Superdome, where they are attached to more cables and wires that flow to every part of the facility: the scoreboard, seats,

THE DEVIL NEVER SLEEPS

parking lot, locker rooms, the field. In games leading to the Super Bowl, the new system was troublesome; there were minor disruptions of energy flow. These were described by stadium manager Doug Thornton as "gremlins" and were worrisome enough that the facility drew out contingency plans should the Superdome lose power. These plans included a public announcement to spectators: "Return to your seats. Stay calm."[7]

In the weeks before the game, the continuing gremlins suggested that the system might not hold for the big event. There would be too much pressure on the grid with the addition of increased press presence and the famous Super Bowl halftime concert. Beyoncé was the scheduled star. As a precaution, just a few days before the big game, the halftime show was sourced by a different power generator.

At halftime on game day, everything seemed fine. Beyoncé strutted to "Crazy in Love" and "Single Ladies." There were no gremlins. But the smoke from her show had to be removed from the field quickly, so the equivalent of air conditioning for outdoor stadiums was amped up. Thornton remembers that as the game restarted, some emails vanished from his phone. "I had this eerie feeling," he told *Sports Illustrated*.[8] Gremlins. A minute and thirty-eight seconds into the third quarter, the lights on the west side of the Superdome vanished. The A feed was lost. Half the Superdome plunged into darkness. Since most people did not know about the previous glitches, the fear of terrorism came to mind.

The B feed was intact. And it had to remain intact. The systems were bifurcated in the layered design of the new post-Katrina Superdome so that a disruption in the A feed would not impact the B feed's capacity. The designers had seen that a single source, as was true at the Superdome during Katrina, can fail fantastically. Other contingency planning that had been put into place—emergency lighting, public communications, text messages to spectators—were activated based on the previous training. Nonessential needs, such as air conditioning, on the B feed were immediately terminated to relieve pressure. The response had been anticipated and practiced. A bank of lights that had been put on a separate system in case the primary system failed were turned on. All of these efforts—separate feeds so one could be managed if the other faltered, contingency planning, taking pressure off the system, backups for emergencies—amounted to a safer failure. And although the Super Bowl was inconvenienced, it did not plunge into full darkness. The lights went to full capacity thirty-four minutes later after a system reboot. The game continued, and Baltimore won. There was silly talk of conspiracies, the blackout viewed as a sophisticated move by the 49ers to stop Baltimore's near blowout. More importantly, however, there was no chaos. Spectators stayed in their seats.

From the perspective of all that could have gone wrong and the panic that could have followed, this was, in the weird world of disaster management, defined as a success based on what bad things didn't happen, a victory of sorts. Later, a review of the facility found that a device known as a relay in the new switchgears was set too low. The relay measures energy and heat levels, and it shuts down a system should it get too heated. There was no problem with the A feed; the relay was miscalculated to shut down at a level that was significantly lower than what it could handle. Proving we can never have enough contingency planning, the relay, put in to serve as an updated last line of defense, in fact failed.[9] But half the Superdome remained lit. Success.

LEARNING FROM ZOMBIES

Conceptually, cascading losses can be understood and worked to eliminate or mitigate harm. The training to do so has been formalized by public safety and public health agencies. But instead of using a bomb or a blackout, they practice for the coming of the undead. Zombie studies are a real thing. In movies and literature, the undead have engaged audiences for centuries. The term itself, *zombie*, refers generically to human corpses that are reanimated to be lifelike, including the capacity to kill. *The Walking Dead* series is a recent example of its modern-day appeal. Beyoncé may be great entertainment for a doomed Super Bowl, but the cultural phenomenon of zombies has been used by crisis managers to help them think through every imaginable contingency that might occur in the event of a catastrophe that is inexplicable. Indeed, one of the reasons zombies are a nice twenty-first-century disaster feature is that they are a protean thread. They keep changing, much like the devil. Early zombie films, like *Night of the Living Dead*, describe zombies as a radiological phenomenon. Later, they were often the product of nuclear weapons or a nuclear accident. More recently, they have become the result of a biological event. The zombie idea is a perfect stand-in for all the things we're concerned about in the twenty-first century.

Zombies know how to survive, a sort of mastery of stopping the bleed. That zombies, apparently dead, still bleed seems to defy the basic biology of what it means to be dead. The blood should stop. Whether it is because they aren't technically dead, but instead undead, or because their blood flow continues due to their capacity to stand and circulate, the fact that zombies don't ever seem to bleed out is a significant controversy in online chatter.[10] Suspending this great debate for a little, even the Centers for Disease Control got into the zombie mania. Well before COVID-19, in 2011, they launched a zombie preparedness effort. It was wildly popular, as it was a fun way, if zombies are your idea of fun, to describe preparedness planning and what one might do to protect yourself: stay at home, shelter in place, have an emergency kit, don't let strangers in (especially if they look dead). The effort expanded to school education materials, a blog, and a web series.[11]

Professor Daniel Drezner, an international politics expert, has made a name as a geopolitical scholar and a zombie expert.[12] He got into the field when he was updating lessons on realpolitik for his college students. He realized that college freshmen were more likely to know about zombies than they were to understand Machiavelli. And in his serious analysis of zombies, he came away with a simple critique: the entire genre discounted human agency to mitigate more damage.

"If there is an overarching narrative to most in the zombie genre, it is that when pressed, human beings will eventually end up acting like zombies. They will be greedy, they will be cynical, that trust in institutions is not terribly well-placed. So one of the interesting things about doing the book was that I wound up concluding that the zombie genre was too pessimistic about humanity," Drezner told me in an interview.[13] The fallacy in the zombie genre is that it assumes much greater agency by the zombies—who could adapt, mitigate, protect themselves—than it did by humans. It underestimates humanity. "We're an awesome species! We invented duct tape, for Christ's sake. We can come up with some things on our own," Drezner concluded.[14]

We did invent duct tape. It is amazing. It stops the cascading losses. The whole zombie genre underestimates humanity and our capacity to have agency to protect ourselves better. The legitimately interesting aspect of the zombie genre is how humans react to each other because of their fear and stress. Most contributions about the zombie genre are quite pessimistic about whether humans have a way to protect themselves better as the apocalypse unfolds. We, humans, all end up dead (or undead).

But it is only when humans actually cooperate, recognize the disaster unfolding, and try to mitigate the harm that things begin to look better. Interestingly, newer contributions to the end-of-times genre—*The Walking Dead* franchise, *Station Eleven*—are based on the lives of a generation of humans that grew up postapocalypse and are living sometime downstream from the initial boom. The human combatants of the future have discovered that their planning and preparedness still matter and they can help limit the scope of the damage. They have agency.

So do we. Too little safe-to-fail effort has gone into our planning and design. This is particularly troublesome when disasters should be anticipated to recur because it takes longer to recover from a crisis based on the amount of damage that has been done. In a world where success is not measured as either/or, stopping more cascading losses can be the ultimate victory. Before the boom, we can prepare in ways that would limit waves and waves of damage. We can, at the very least, try to stop the bleed. Sometimes, of course, there are no alternatives, and the damage is done. But that is only rarely the case.

"STUPID DEATHS"

The reasons planning needs to address cascading losses, failing safer, and stopping the bleed are written in the casualty count. If the damage cascades—driving increased fatalities, public health harms, and property damage—the length of the catastrophe will also delay recovery efforts, making it longer and harder for communities to rebound successfully. As time passes, more damage will come.

Puerto Rican authorities knew this, for example, well before Hurricane Maria struck the island in 2017.[15] They understood that an electric system that relied on a single, vulnerable grid could be wiped out by a single bad storm. And it was. They tried to get the US—Puerto Rico's territorial status impacts its ability to control its destiny—to help build better systems, mostly by diversifying its grid system so that they could better control losses. It was never done. After Maria hit the island, electricity was out for weeks and, in some areas, months.

To this day, we do not know how many people died during Hurricane Maria. The death estimate has ranged, and that is the consequence of a simple fact: most of the deaths were not related to the hurricane itself, but to the downstream consequences of the power outage. Without electricity, deprivations of water, food, and medicines left people vulnerable. More people died than should have. These cases have a name: "stupid deaths." This is the term Haitians, survivors of so many disasters, have given to fatalities that occur because people can't get basic needs addressed as the disaster's impact keeps cascading.[16]

They would know. The Haiti earthquake in 2010 devastated the country and left more than 250,000 dead. The country was already deeply poor with a limited infrastructure to prevent excess deaths. And help from abroad was limited by a simple fact: only one runway remained viable in the capital's airport at Port-au-Prince once the morning sun came up after the magnitude 7.0 earthquake struck. There is a lot of debate about how Haiti and the international community responded, much of it focusing on the decision to allow ten thousand US troops in first. It was looked at warily, as Haiti is a country well aware of military intervention from the US in the past. The media and NGOs, like Doctors Without Borders, pushed for greater access to address other priorities, including the many orphans created by the quake that killed their parents.

What Haiti knew, and what the US Army certainly understood, is that without food and water, whatever Haiti was experiencing would become much worse. The single runway was handed over to the US, which managed air control by putting three soldiers on a single table who directed traffic by visual cues and binoculars. The planes came in and out, in intervals never experienced before, about one every minute. The army has unique talents, and delivering meals to avoid anarchy is one. The troops dispersed throughout the country, building food and water tents and delivery positions, to beat any anarchy. What seemed cruel, making the orphans finding homes in the US a secondary priority, had an important rationale. Haiti's government wanted to stop as many deaths as possible in the weeks after the earthquake.

Stupid deaths can also occur without any physical harm. Hamako Watanabe, a fifty-eight-year-old woman, was evacuated from her home after the 2011 Fukushima disaster. Then a massive earthquake created an equally massive tsunami that flooded the Daiichi nuclear power plant in Okuma, Fukushima.[17] The first two disasters—an earthquake and tsunami—are not preventable. The nuclear facility's meltdown was, and the radiation caused by negligent preparedness was a downstream failure. Radiation was released, and Japan evacuated thousands of residents. Watanabe and her husband, Mikio, lived just twenty-five miles from the power plant, so their home was part of an extensive planned evacuation zone. The couple, older, drifted for months after, during which time Hamako's mental state deteriorated. She came to know she would never return to her home. Later, and only for a few hours, evacuees were allowed access to reclaim their necessities. As her husband organized and packed the house, he smelled and then heard a fire in the yard. Hamako had set herself aflame near a garbage incinerator at the home. Was her death due to Fukushima? Hard to say it wasn't. Was it a stupid death? There are arguments both ways. But more than sixty people committed suicide related to the impact of the quake and tsunami, according to records from the Japanese government. Mikio Watanabe sued TEPCO, the energy company, viewing their negligence as a proximate cause of the suicide, as clear as if radiation had slowly seeped through her body and destroyed her organs. He won in court.[18]

It would be erroneous to think that the suicide was just another loss, like so many, that day. The nuclear facility had every capacity to stop the cascading damage. It had not planned for it to be on the receiving end of a series of totally predictable natural disasters. But the damage it caused was not due to the earthquake or tsunami. It was entirely because its response was inadequate. While the name Fukushima is now well known, few talk of the Onagawa Nuclear Power Station managed by Tohoku Electric Power Company in the same vicinity. Onagawa, which had felt the "strongest shaking that any nuclear plant has ever experienced from an earthquake," according to a report by the International Atomic Energy Agency, did not falter.[19] Because of design, planning, and a safety culture that recognized that a disaster of this magnitude might come, Onagawa was able to minimize the losses, and there were no radiation leaks. It "shut down safely."[20]

EXTEND THE RUNWAY

In 1906, the philosopher and author Alfred Henry Lewis stated that "there are only nine meals between mankind and anarchy."[21] The refrain would be repeated by the likes of Leon Trotsky and Robert Heinlein; there is a 2018 disaster movie with the same name. We can live without shoes and hairstylists, but if we go too long without food, then people act in all sorts of destabilizing ways. More people will die. The sentiment drives how we ought to think about response planning. We have nine meals of time.

Conceptually, think of it as trying to extend the runway. The phrase describes how longer distances to take off and land a plane provide a safety buffer for pilots. For the most part, a lot of the efforts described in this book are about the same goal: buying ourselves some time to avoid greater harm. *Less bad*, so to speak. It is a matter of creating systems that can be built on each other, layered like molasses, to delay catastrophic failure for as long as possible in the hopes that delay will actually make catastrophe less consequential. Security investments, like better situational awareness and sophisticated training, are efforts that ultimately provide more time to try different options during a disaster.

We try to extend the runway in many facets of life without really calling it that. Small businesses, strapped for cash, find ways to remain viable when money is running low. Rebudgeting, laying off employees, getting rid of contractors, or giving up on an expensive real estate footprint and going remote help put money back in the bank and let the company survive for longer.[22] It's a way of making sure the company doesn't crash and burn. More recently, during the pandemic in

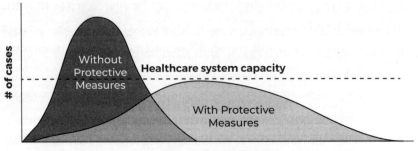

Flattening the curve.

those early days of lockdown, our stated goal to "flatten the curve" was really about giving ourselves more time. A flattened curve, after all, is a longer one.

This familiar image is telling. It isn't about stopping the virus; it is about slowing it. In both pandemic scenarios shown here, with or without protective measures, the number of cases is the same. Flattening the curve was instead about pacing. It was about avoiding a catastrophic breakdown of our hospital systems that would have become—indeed, did become—overwhelmed when too many people showed up at the same time. By staying inside, we hoped to slow the demand placed on the hospitals, ensuring that they had the capacity to address needs or at least allowing for alternatives such as makeshift medical facilities. Flattening the curve, if we did it right, which we didn't, was meant to give us time to avoid the catastrophe of a devastated medical system, unable to help those with or without COVID-19 who needed hospital care.

The boom happens, but so much more is still to come: bleeding out, potential full blackouts, and stupid deaths. On a personal level, with our kids or communities, we have to let ourselves go to that bad place in our heads where the zombies are in order to figure out where we can assert agency. A helpful exercise to minimize cascading losses is to think of effective disaster management as akin to a block of swiss cheese. A lot of planners like this Emmenthal metaphor. The goal is never to have the holes align and therefore be able to see to the other side; counterintuitively, you want to avoid the light. We want to design a complicated system in ways where the failures can fail more safely so that we can keep pivoting and delaying, pivoting and delaying, again and again, before the cascading losses multiply and gain momentum and we can never stop the bleed.

The devil has plenty of time. We can always benefit from a longer runway. Build it now. You are here.

CHAPTER SIX

THE WAY WE WERE

Buildings Don't Just Fall

On June 24, 2021, the Champlain Towers South condominium complex near Miami collapsed in the middle of the night, crushing more than one hundred sleeping residents. The catastrophe was shocking.[1] Buildings, for the most part, don't just fall down without some external event: an explosion or earthquake. It is rare for a building just to crumble. When daylight came, everyone could see a building half collapsed, the other side teetering, wires and concrete exposing the innards of a structure that was now the deathbed for so many. What happened? Was it the pool? The garage? Construction on the roof?

For years, the structure was known to be at risk. Three years before the collapse, a consulting firm that assessed the building warned of "major structural damage" to the concrete slab below the pool deck as well as to the walls and beams of the underground parking garage. "The main issue with this building structure is that the entrance drive/pool deck/planter waterproofing is laid on a flat structure," the firm, Maryland-based Morabito Consultants, wrote to the condo association. "Since the reinforced concrete slab is not sloped to drain, the water sits on the waterproofing until it evaporates."[2] Why Champlain Towers South collapsed that night was the cumulative impact of a lot of factors. What triggers a catastrophe may be something small,

Champlain Tower South in Surfside, Florida, after collapse.

but it is aligned at the right moment with all sorts of other small (and big) deficiencies. In the weeks and months after the collapse, we learned that regulations were often not enforced, the Champlain Towers residential board was slow to move, and even climate change and the changing composition of the soil contributed to its downfall.

In a thorough investigation done by the *Wall Street Journal*, the question "What happened?" results in only one answer: everything. It was a cumulative pattern of neglect that could not withstand changing circumstances. The planning and construction of the high-rise met most building codes from forty years ago, but those choices would eventually meet the climate in 2021. Shoreline shifts and climate change were known to increase rust accumulation and expand concrete slabs by consistent exposure to saltwater. This makes concrete crack. By the early 1980s, when the Champlain Towers were built, the American Concrete Institute already was advising clients to better waterproof building slabs by placing "waterproofing membranes" around them.[3] It was never mandated, so the saltwater was never addressed.

As the earth changed, so did the tower's capacity to stand. Not even the smallest of investments that might have stabilized the vulnerable pool area or fortified the garage structure was made. It was all too hard, it seemed, so it wasn't done at all. Maybe they just thought, as we all once did, that buildings don't just fall.

But if conditions change, buildings do just fall.

SUNK COSTS

Safety and security systems are designed based on conditions as they existed when they were built. We come to believe that those conditions are constant because there is no compelling reason for us to think otherwise. The features, be it a padlock or a sophisticated cybersecurity network, have worked in the past, so why shouldn't they continue to work? Nothing bad has happened so far, after all. But fundamentals are always changing. That is the nature of the devil; if the threat were always the same, we would have this disaster management stuff figured out by now. The Champlain Towers, after all, were made more unstable by increased moisture in the soil and rain on the roof, both the result of changes to the sea level and temperatures due to climate change. Similarly, terrorists change their motivations and methods. Cyber criminals alter their methods to avert security systems in place. Hurricanes get stronger and linger longer. And so on and so forth.

Preparation for the boom is never complete, especially when doom can come any day, every day. This should translate into a constant reassessment, revamping, or maybe just tinkering of the security that is in place to determine whether the assumptions the system is based on still hold. Too often, I've seen institutions, in good faith, build effective preparedness measures—they commit to unity of effort, strong situational awareness, avoid the last line of defense planning—but then let them linger as time passes them by. They felt they were done, as if disasters were still random and rare.

Part of this conduct is likely explained by the sunk cost fallacy. The term *sunk cost* comes from the field of economics, sometimes called a retrospective cost. It describes an investment that has already been put into an effort that can no longer be recovered. The fallacy arises when the mere fact of that investment justifies continuing the same behavior regardless of whether that behavior is still warranted because the resources are committed. We do not consider whether the effort is still a good investment because we have already invested time and money. This is what it means to throw good money after bad. The investments already made justify themselves simply because they have been made.

The sunk cost fallacy applies to the security world as well. The Vietnam War is a pretty brutal example. "The decision you face now is crucial," the senior State Department official George Ball wrote to President Lyndon Johnson in 1965 as Johnson sought more resources for the war. "Once large numbers of US troops are committed to direct combat, they will begin to take heavy casualties in a war they are ill equipped to fight in a noncooperative if not downright hostile countryside. Once we suffer large casualties, we will have started a well-nigh irreversible process."[4] Nevertheless, Johnson continued the campaign, each investment of soldiers and money becoming the reason for continuing the same path. The locking in of resources blinds the decision maker to both the limitations of the original investment and any alternatives to success, or at least a managed defeat.

The sunk cost fallacy has another name; it is sometimes referred to as the *Concorde fallacy*. Britain and France, in a 1976 collaboration, committed to building the supersonic passenger jet. It was expensive and suffered safety setbacks, and few aviation companies were seeking orders. It was not at all clear how the countries would recoup their investment. Nonetheless, they persisted, throwing more and more money because they were already so far in. They just kept building a plane that wasn't quite right. On July 25, 2000, Air France Concorde Flight 4590 crashed, killing 113 people. It was a tragedy, but it finally forced a course correction. The companies dropped any future plans for development of more planes.

The fallacy assumes that there is a single static investment that holds over time. Sustained preparedness is a necessary rejoinder to the preparedness paradox, but that does not mean our planning remains static. Instead, it is better to think of the appropriate level of preparedness as a moving target. There is no finish line. One helpful conceptual tool is to think about right-of-boom planning as a three-legged stool that is constantly readjusting to the circumstances of an uneven floor. What we are trying to do, professionally and personally, is constantly stabilize the stool. Prior investments may have been worth it at a certain moment in time but probably not for the end of times.

THE GROUND SHIFTS

Terrorists want a lot of people watching, but not a lot of people dead. That insight guided almost all counterterrorism efforts and response planning for decades. The assumption was that the terrorists had some political goal and that killing a large number of harmless civilians indiscriminately would be counterproductive. It was believed that a high death count would alienate the public against the terror group, and what the terror group wanted most was public support of their efforts. At least that was the assumption.

The evidence was clear in the late 1990s and 2000 that this was no longer the case. The rise of al-Qaeda was documented by intelligence agencies throughout the world. Al-Qaeda was no longer following the old playbook that guided groups like the Irish Republican Army or Germany's Baader-Meinhof Gang. Al-Qaeda had made its intentions clear, and the bombing of two US embassies in Africa in 1998, followed by the attack on the USS *Cole* in Yemen in 2000, were all the proof that should have been needed.

Looking back at what was missed, the 9/11 Commission would famously call America's lack of preparation, among other things, a "failure of imagination."[5] I never liked that term, as it makes it seem that there was some unknowable, unimaginable scenario that didn't occur to the American government. Later, released documents would expose that a lot was already known about al-Qaeda. On January 25, 2001, in the first days of the Bush administration, Richard Clarke, a career terrorism expert on the national security staff, sent a warning to the new national security advisor, Condoleezza Rice. The memo laid out the growing concern among experts about, as he spelled it at the time, "al Qida." The first heading, put in question form, was somewhat rhetorical: "Just Some Terrorist Group?" The answer was obviously no. "As we noted in our briefings for you," Clarke wrote, "al Qida is not some narrow, little terrorist issue. . . . al Qida is the active, organized, major force that is using a distorted version of Islam as its vehicle."[6] But US efforts were stuck in a planning scenario that assumed terrorists could be understood, that our sense of rationality was their sense of rationality.

It wasn't about imagination; it was about assuming the lessons of the past were preparation for the future. The data and intelligence indicated that the narrative had changed. Al-Qaeda was bragging about plans for a catastrophic attack on American soil targeting civilians. If those messages had been taken seriously, there might have been an attempt to stop them. But there might have also been an attempt to mitigate the consequences—the right of boom—when nineteen terrorists entered four planes on the morning of September 11, 2001.

Airlines were not notified of a potential threat. No warning went specifically to pilots, who are trained for a hostage situation. No twenty-five-dollar locks were put on the cockpit doors to secure them from incursions from the main cabin. No message was shared with the Federal Aviation Agency or other government entities that might be impacted. Only the passengers on United Airlines Flight 93 had any information about what had happened to the other flights. They congregated at the back of the plane and voted to attempt to take over the cockpit to avert catastrophe, as the terrorists were likely heading toward a government building in the nation's capital. The plane went down near Shanksville, Pennsylvania, just about 120 miles from the White House.[7]

We can only learn so much from the past. It may give hints of what is to come, but the exact contours of how a disaster unfolds is rarely going to follow a script. History is relevant, but it may too often serve as an impediment to effective consequence management. We are tied to a notion of how things will unfold so that our response efforts are viewed as adequate because they were once good enough. Just because a response was good enough to handle the last disaster, that doesn't mean it is ready for the next one. The military analogy is the general who prepares to fight the last war. History can guide and expose, but it can also imprison. Society and institutions are much better at adapting to the last crisis than preparing for the next one.

This is often because systems are generally established in the aftermath of a significant crisis, when the pain and harm of recent events are fresh in leaders' and citizens' minds. In the aftermath of 9/11, for example, the United States reconfigured its entire homeland security apparatus, passed new laws to allocate more resources and attention to antiterrorism efforts, and entered multiple forever wars without clear goals or objectives. Since then, inordinate amounts of resources have been devoted to counterterrorism efforts, which, while important, often distracted from numerous *other* security vulnerabilities that have more recently been revealed: a weak public health infrastructure, exposure to the climate crisis and the increasing frequency of natural disasters, a polarized civic society that is increasingly susceptible to widespread disinformation, domestic terror, and more. However, the country's crisis orientation often remains rigidly focused on its remembrance of the *last* crisis.

A recurrent disaster management system must adapt to new and entirely unexpected events rather than expect a predictable repetition of the past. And that means that whatever system of response—right-of-boom—capabilities that has been established represents just a moment in time, a reflection tied to that instance, and needs to be constantly and consistently revised based on intelligence, evidence, or even just a gut feeling.

History is, in some ways, the sunk cost here. It creates a blinding myopia for the past. Jim Clapper, former head of National Intelligence, described the dangers as "if it hasn't happened yet, it isn't likely to happen."[8] In changing times of recurring disasters, we can never be too confident. Confidence may be a good attribute for a leader, but not for a crisis manager. It leads to laziness, a sense that "we got this." We can learn from history but be prepared for a different dance next time.

IT SNOWS IN TEXAS

This confidence that the past is prologue creates an inertia in response planning that is inadequate for the future. In 2021, a fluke winter storm put the whole state of Texas into subfreezing temperatures. Its electricity infrastructure quickly became overwhelmed, and a massive power outage followed. The weather impacted every single way that electricity was delivered: coal, wind, natural gas, and nuclear. At the crisis's worst moment, up to 4.5 million homes and businesses were in the dark.[9]

Texas had planned for such a contingency; ice storms were not new. But an ice storm that impacted the entire state was not a contingency planned for because it had never happened before. Sure, some systems could go down, and Texas could pull from one region of the state to another, diverting within its own boundaries. They had every reason to believe that was enough because it had worked before. It is Texas, after all.

Texans waiting for provisions after 2021 winter storm. Source: Tamir Kalifa, *New York Times*.

America's energy delivery system is not just the combination of two contiguous American electrical power grids, one for the east and the other for the west. There is a third: the Electric Reliability Council of Texas (ERCOT). Why is Texas so special? In 1935, Roosevelt signed the Federal Power Act, which gave the US authority to regulate interstate power lines. Much like the federal highway program, Roosevelt used the powers of the Constitution's Commerce Clause to unify a country's basic needs and create interstate capacity. Texas wanted no part of it. It had already created its own grid, so it backed out of Roosevelt's plan; if it didn't join national efforts, it thought, then it couldn't be regulated. ERCOT, which was formally established in 1970, remained outside the jurisdiction of the Federal Energy Regulatory Commission. Much as Texas views itself as a country on its own, ERCOT—with some minor exceptions—is isolated. Those exceptions are "kind of a drop in the bucket, but there are those minor connections. That aside, we do operate electrically as an island," ERCOT president and CEO Bill Magness told the *Texas Tribune* before he was fired after the storm.[10]

An isolated response capability built when FDR was president is no system at all. That Texas might need to access grids from either the east or west was never part of the planning because an entire state faltering had no historical precedent. Buildings, in other words, don't just fall. Texas had, to its credit, tested diversions within the state; flow more to Dallas or Lubbock or wherever if the need should arise. That's what companies do. But it couldn't see past the reality that climate patterns would eventually change and that there might be a circumstance Texas couldn't handle on its own. Conservative politicians in the state might not like the term *climate change*, but citizens like their heat.

I once asked Miles O'Brien, a well-known space and climate reporter, how it is that smart people are incapable of seeing the changes occurring around them. He spoke of groupthink and static planning. "It's more a story of how a collective group of smart people can, at the sum total, be dumber than the parts."[11] After I tweeted O'Brien's comment, a follower wrote back: "None of us is as dumb as all of us."[12]

WHERE IS THE LIEUTENANT GOVERNOR?

The best way to ensure that the planning in place today can adapt to the future is to continuously stress test the system. This is where a notion called red teaming comes in handy. Red teaming is a terminology that comes from military war-gaming. It is done to challenge plans, policies, and assumptions by opening up to a potential adversary who wants you dead (figuratively). The military sets up an OPFOR—opposing force—in a fictional conflict that challenges the conventional wisdom of planning and activities. The aggressor serves as a test against the "defenders"—the blue team—who are unaware of what the red team plans. The enemy's capabilities, weapons, and techniques may be entirely new. In the military, the red team is a purposeful, determined enemy. The exercise itself is a way of providing alternative analysis, a break from the expectations of the past. Red teaming can be "real" in the sense that both teams physically move in response to each other. In this way, operational issues—like how long it actually takes to cover thirty yards while carrying a heavy load—are put under the microscope.

The red-teaming effort can be used outside the military. It does not have to apply to warfare. Work or community teams can sit around a table and talk through different responses based on a hypothetical scenario. This can prove valuable—and less costly. Planning and communicating about expectations can expose faulty assumptions and help teams adapt. This option is called a tabletop exercise. This is when an outside group, a red team, will help an institution determine the success of its response planning. During this effort, the key players are directed to react to various scenarios in a simulation that is constantly changing based on decisions already made. A good tabletop will challenge assumptions but also throw in random events. This technique is often used in the cybersecurity context and is known as a penetration exercise or test. Here companies will hire hackers— who they euphemistically call *ethical hackers*—to use every resource they have in order to hack into the computer system. The difference from a real-life scenario, however, is that the blue team, so to speak, actually knows that the hackers are coming; surprise is taken out of the test. Instead, the goal is to see if the company can mount any defense and mitigate any damage.

These efforts cannot be underestimated. They add purposeful variation to preparedness, as they challenge any lazy planning that says that success is just doing more of the same. Of course, the red teams, for example, can identify vulnerabilities, which is always helpful for the left side of the boom. Exposing weaknesses on the front end can decrease the likelihood of needing investments on the back end. But most importantly, these tests can expose where response systems are lacking.

One of my favorite—can I call it that?—red-teaming efforts was when we tested a state government's capabilities. Much of their planning revolved around the efforts and leadership of the governor himself. He's the boss, his staff thought. This phenomenon of thinking the principal will rise to the occasion isn't unusual, but it has one tremendous flaw: the potential that an attack would impact the governor himself. The way that the state had planned its response management left the constitutional successor—the lieutenant governor—outside most of the exercises and training. So within a few minutes of the test exercise, we made the governor a victim of the hurricane that they had trained for. We "drowned" him. The remaining senior government officials looked around the room. "Where's the lieutenant governor?" somebody asked. Nobody had invited the lieutenant governor. Big problem.

Keep testing, and don't get lulled.[13] The red-teaming effort provides a new set of eyes looking at structures and planning and wondering, in fact, testing, whether the old eyes got everything just right. Outsiders brought in can have a way of making sure insiders don't rely too much on testing the weak spots they already know. In cybersecurity, for example, internal business tests often will poke and probe at the same place where they already know there are weaknesses. Ethical hackers will get them out of that comfort zone. It isn't as if large technology companies don't test their systems, after all, but they tend to protect the scab; it just takes the outsider to rip it off.

Every system has to be stress tested, continuously. That is the nature of sustained preparedness. We've succeeded in convincing a majority of society that climate change is happening but have been less successful in getting them to focus on how they should plan for any response. The past is telling us that things may get worse, but how they will do so is unknown.

THE SAFETY OFFSET

An additional reason the preparedness system put into place at home or in the world should be regularly tested is a cautionary phenomenon called risk homeostasis, RHT. Basically, not only do the circumstances of the world change, such as weather, but so do we. As leaders and institutions become committed to preparing for disasters, there can be a tendency to counteract those investments with more risky behavior.

RHT theory was initially proposed by Queen's University professor emeritus Gerald Wilde to explain why some safety measures were not resulting in the overall net benefit anticipated.[14] This isn't to say precautionary efforts like helmets, for example, don't help, only that skiers who wear helmets are more likely to go faster and therefore increase the likelihood of harm.[15] Since Wilde's findings in 1982, there has been criticism of some of his methodology. But this theory of risk compensation helps explain why some safety interventions may yield fewer benefits than anticipated. People often adjust their behavior in response to the initial safety investment. Essentially, do we become less careful if we feel that there is a safety net to protect us from our mistakes?

Wilde examined a variety of safety measures and initiatives and argued that they often do not work out as planned because of subjective risk perceptions. RHT posits that individuals and institutions will evaluate risk, altering their safety effectiveness, to achieve a certain level of risk, known as the target level of risk. RHT explains what might be called risk offsets, the tendency to push the envelope as more and more safety measures come into place. The evidence for it is sometimes controversial—surely, we know safety measures do work, but RHT tries to explain why they might not work as well as we think.[16]

Conversely, there is also evidence that the lack of safety measures may make us more cautious. This has been the overall data from urban areas that have adopted shared space street design. In these areas, signals, road surface markings, and even curbs are removed. The sensation of feeling unsafe resulted in fewer accidents. "It may seem perverse to argue that well-being can be improved through making spaces feel riskier," wrote the authors of a major study on open-space design, "but that is the firm conclusion from" the empirical studies.[17]

Our agency is not always a force for good if we use it to offset the very investments that make us safer. Skydiving legend Bill Booth has an eye-opening explanation for this. Known as Booth's rule #2, he says that "the safer skydiving gear becomes, the more chances skydivers will take, in order to keep the fatality rate constant."[18] Indeed, despite all the significant changes—including safety devices—the skydiving death rate hasn't changed. Parachutes have become safer, but also faster and more complicated, with high-performing canopies making divers overconfident because of the safety features. They try high-speed maneuvers closer to the ground, which sometimes do not work. What this all means is that planners and leaders have to be cognizant of the safety measures' effects, as they might result in a risk tolerance in response to new rules or engineering technologies.

RHT reminds us of our capacity to do stupid things, that after we commit to being prepared, we may blow it all on a risky skydiving maneuver. It warns us that we have to overcome the tendency to view embracing the right side of the boom as creating an opportunity to offset its benefits. That potential offset can be exposed through these same exercises and stress tests.

IN THE THICK OF IT

As highlighted above, before the real-life event, disaster management benefits from red team and tabletop exercises that can challenge assumptions about how an event might unfold. As will be noted in chapter 8, after the real-life event, disaster management benefits from after-action reports and historical memorialization so that the correct lessons can be learned. That leaves a third category of learning: lessons to be adapted during the event, in the thick of it. Here, disaster management is undergoing a significant shift in an era of catastrophes. Essentially, since the disasters are recurring, the benefits of learning in real time, and not just before and after, are immeasurable.

Lessons anticipated or learned have a static feel to them, as if the best learning comes only with foresight or hindsight.

"But what if a failed project could have been more successful if only there had been some reviews along the way, at the end of each step or phase, that would have impacted the end?" professors Marilyn Darling, Charles Parry, and Joseph Moore write in a seminal article in *Harvard Business Review* called "Learning in the Thick of It."[19] In other words, by adapting to what is learned in real time, the future may be written differently. They describe a lessons-learned process that is actually living and moving. Their study researched why teams facing an OPFOR enemy were so successful, mainly that they never seemed to be surprised. What the researchers determined is that learning was continuous, even during the crisis. During the exercise, the blue team set up a cycle of midbattle meetings that focused on operational orders and whether they were still working for the mission at hand. This process helped reform and refine the team in the moment rather than in the future. And they focused not only on what went right, but also on whether what went right will continue to go right under different circumstances, such as completing a mission at night or with new technology.[20]

This process of "learning in the thick of it" began as part of military training and was later adopted by major corporations and institutions. By the late 1990s, it made its way to project management tools. Project management is now familiar to any business student. Its expansion to the business sector is often identified with General Gordon Sullivan (Ret.), who served on the board of Shell Oil. He suggested that the company utilize the OPFOR training as a business tool to more efficiently identify best practices and mistakes before they got too far along in any project. These management changes would permanently transform business practices by identifying errors and remedying glitches before a project got too far along. Why shouldn't institutions of any size be willing to reform during the onboarding of new technology, a payroll management system, or a supply-chain logistics process as well as during a disaster or crisis? We should.

OCCUPY THIS

Hurricane Sandy—often referred to as Superstorm Sandy, describing several storms wrapped together—was the most destructive and deadliest hurricane of the 2012 Atlantic season. It killed 233 people across eight countries, from the Caribbean to Canada. Although it was only a Category 2 hurricane by the time it hit the United States, it was the largest Atlantic hurricane measured by tropical-storm-force winds; it spanned 1,150 miles, the largest diameter on record. In the US, the hurricane affected nearly half the states, a geographic impact that is mind-boggling. On October 29, it hit New York City, leaving death and damage in its wake, flooding the streets, and cutting power in and around the city. Nearly five thousand airline flights were canceled, and Amtrak suspended rail services. Sandy was like no other hurricane.

Previous planning was a good baseline, as federal, state, and local authorities prepared communities for the disaster. But Sandy passed through and left in its wake unprecedented devastation that had to be responded to, recorded, and understood. The scale of Sandy and the needs in the immediate response were overwhelming. Much of public response planning had not yet adapted to bigger storms, let alone new technology and new politics. The needs were too great to apply the same rules.

It was, coincidentally, also the time of Occupy Wall Street, the grassroots efforts by communities to make income inequality—through protests and sit-ins—a public policy priority. They had a few things that would be useful in an emergency, such as neighborhood knowledge and a commitment to making things better. Occupy Wall Street members tended to be younger, technologically adept, and able to put together spreadsheets and Google Docs faster than most. When Hurricane Sandy came, the Occupy Wall Street people had to disperse to protect themselves and get into shelter. When the storm finally passed, Occupy Sandy was born.

It was an impromptu gig.[21] Some veterans of Occupy Wall Street started to organize and deliver food and flashlights to housing projects in Brooklyn. It then took off. They used Twitter to get new volunteers and organized cars to transport commodities and goods. They became a rapid response team of sorts. It meant money quickly got into the hands of people and businesses that needed it, families were sent to shelters faster, and relief was made more accessible to immigrant and minority communities due to a greater understanding of community needs.

The Occupy Sandy experiment has been replicated in disasters since, though it has shed the *Occupy* name. The government, recognizing that storms were getting bigger and more frequent, could no longer rely on previous planning, which treated most communities as victims rather than as survivors who had the capacity to help. This effort mirrored a whole-of-community approach to disaster response that the government was already implementing under programs like FEMA corps, a new national program for eighteen- to twenty-four-year-olds. Richard Serino, the deputy administrator of FEMA at the time, told me that Superstorm Sandy was the first really successful use of local ingenuity in disaster response. "Community groups like Occupy Sandy, as well as many others, highlighted that community groups are part of the solution." In an age of disasters, these new efforts "have not only made the experience better for survivors but have also transformed how FEMA utilizes technology in the field," Serino noted, reflecting on how constant innovation affects those in need and those providing help. The danger continues to change. So must our response.[22]

The devil will keep moving. You are no longer back there. You are here.

CHAPTER SEVEN

THE NEAR MISS FALLACY

Can You Hear Me Now?

In June 2010, the iPhone 4 was launched with much fanfare. Soon after, customers were going online to publicly denounce its signal strength. Lots of people were experiencing dropped calls and interrupted messaging. Apple responded in the worst way possible: blaming how customers held the phone or, as former CEO Steve Jobs wrote, describing it as a "nonissue." Eventually, Apple admitted the software failures and sought to remedy the errors for a phone that had failed to get even a recommendation from *Consumer Reports*. That Apple's initial response—which drew withering condemnation and even a lawsuit—was pathetic and defensive is well known now. What isn't more commonly known is how unsurprising the complaints were.

For Apple, the iPhone must work. There is no other product line so vital to the company. So what was wrong with the iPhone 4 that had not bedeviled previous versions? Turns out, nothing. The Apple official response would later explain that "gripping any phone will result in some attenuation of its antenna performance with certain places being worse than others depending on the placement of the antennas."[1] This particular error existed in previous iPhones. But for some reason, even though the company knew it, customers never complained and accepted the flaw. It was social media, an aggressive variable, that doomed the iPhone 4. An annoyance for one customer became a groundswell that soon became a major flaw threatening Apple's most successful product.[2]

The fact that customers had already experienced the flaw, however, wasn't a sign that everything was fine; it was only a sign that customers would tolerate a certain amount of annoyance until they couldn't any longer. Apple had normalized the problem, and therefore the public did as well. The dropped calls were near misses, not outliers. Those near misses tell us something that needs to be heard. They are often hints that the system has a default, an error, that if not corrected could lead to a great unraveling. For right-of-boom purposes and the goal of consequence minimization, the near misses aren't necessarily a sign that the system is working. Normalizing them gives institutions and the general public a false sense that the system itself is resilient and the dam can always hold.

Can you hear me now? Things will not hold.

NORMALIZATION OF DEVIANCE

Normalization of deviance is the tendency to ignore near misses rather than acknowledge them as red-siren warnings that the system may be facing a meltdown.[3] The phenomenon of normalization of deviance is important in the disaster management field. The phrase was first coined by the sociologist Diane Vaughan based on her work in studying business and institutional failures.[4] Her findings looked at the time before disasters when the company or team should have known that doom was coming. Why did companies and government entities so readily ignore what, in hindsight, were obvious hints that something was disastrously wrong? She viewed the "near misses" less as a sign that the catastrophe was avoided and more that the catastrophe was waiting to happen.

Like other scholars, Vaughan was drawn to the space shuttle *Challenger* disaster. She, too, was focused on the O-ring, the event we now

Normalization of Deviance

Gradual process through which unacceptable practice or standards become acceptable.

know was the trigger for the explosion.[5] But she didn't stop there. The O-ring was one of hundreds of instances in the buildup of the *Challenger* launch that were hinting, maybe even screaming, of systematic flaws. Each of them was sidelined by the NASA engineers and leaders. Each was normalized.

That normalization occurred because none of them, alone, caused immediate harm. The deviances were superficially benign. Vaughan describes, in her examination of catastrophes, "a long incubation period with early warning signs that were either misinterpreted, ignored or missed completely."[6] While the O-ring was the catastrophic failure, it was not to blame alone. Indeed, the ability to sideline the O-ring's limitations was a sign of a bigger problem. It was ignored because the "boundaries defining acceptable behavior incrementally widened, incorporating incident after aberrant incident."[7] The normalization of deviance is that "gradual process through which unacceptable practice or standards become acceptable. As the deviant behavior is repeated without catastrophic results, it becomes the social norm for the organization."[8] The obvious warnings are dismissed because they don't immediately cause harm. This is the near miss fallacy.

In earlier chapters, I describe how we might all build better response structures for the inevitable boom and what we can do to minimize consequences as it unfolds. *Less bad* is our twenty-first-century standard. In these next two chapters, I focus on how near and recurring disasters actually illuminate opportunities for learning and preparation. They can also provide important feedback as we prepare for the next disaster. This is how Vaughan essentially describes the near miss fallacy. The language should sound familiar, as it aligns with the left- and right-of-boom framework. If an event, a near miss, does not immediately cause a catastrophe, then that near miss begins to be viewed as normal instead. But these near misses are only buying time before the "final disaster," such as the O-ring disintegrating. As we know now, there will inevitably be a final disaster; the devil will return.

How an institution becomes so arrogant, or careless, or simply succumbs to groupthink varies depending on its culture and history. As a whole, institutions suffer from the assumption that the devil isn't lurking; they focus on results (which may be good) rather than mistakes in the system that may be alerts to a potential error. We need to listen to the near misses because they are telling us that we are, more often than not, about as close to the right side of the boom as we ever want to be. We shouldn't feel relief. We should, however, be grateful because the time we now have can help us get ready.

The disruptions described below reframe the conventional wisdom about these crises. In these cases, institutions were open to learning from prior near disasters to avert the most damaging consequences of the next one. They show how institutions learned from disasters that did not happen—in each instance, events could have been so much worse—to avoid catastrophes that seemed likely.

WHAT'S IN THOSE TACOS?

In 2015, sixty cases of *E. coli* were linked to fast-food chain Chipotle's lettuce. It is difficult, to say the least, to run restaurants that are poisoning people. Chipotle was a fast-growing chain; by 2015, it had more than nineteen hundred locations based on a marketing campaign that spoke of the evils of industrial eating. Soon, its market valuation was nearly $24 billion, based on the pitch that fast food and healthy were compatible—or maybe not. *E. coli* in lettuce is bad. Chipotle had a problem in its supply chain that was a reputation-ruining challenge. By the end of the outbreak, five hundred people had become sick from contaminated food. That number represents only those who went to a doctor and provided a sample. Over the course of the crisis, Chipotle lost about 30 percent of its valuation.

Such a massive *E. coli* outbreak, from Oregon to New York, meant that the contamination had occurred at one of the chain's big suppliers. *E. coli* resides in fresh or undercooked foods; it cannot survive high temperatures. For Chipotle, this scientific fact meant that the very attributes that made it unique—the freshness in tomatoes, cilantro, or lettuce—were the culprit.[9] Chipotle now had a real problem, but it reacted successfully, mostly because the company had taken previous near misses seriously. It had heeded those previous warnings. Chipotle was well positioned to respond to a massive *E. coli* outbreak. In the past, it had treated each and every customer complaint or sick employee as the sign of a potential catastrophic incident. When the major *E. coli* breakout hit, Chipotle was ready.

I'm not here to defend an *E. coli* outbreak; clearly it shouldn't have happened. But the company's admittedly self-serving sentiment—that the bottom line could not survive questions by its customers about the safety of its product—drove a sophisticated response that mitigated much of its physical and economic harm. It closed more stores than were necessary, worked cooperatively with the CDC, acted overly cautious and conservative, and quickly restructured their food safety procedures.[10] The company certainly tripped, but it did not fall. Chipotle made massive changes to its protocols for vendor and employee safety. It went public with those changes. It fessed up to its past vulnerabilities. It protected its brand. In 2021, the company had a value of $54 billion, making it one of the world's top four hundred most valuable companies.[11]

BIG SHIP, SMALL CANAL

The company Evergreen's *Ever Given* is one of the world's biggest ships. Much to the glee of comics and GIF creators everywhere, it got wedged in the Suez Canal in March 2021. A wind shift, a bad maneuver, and the boat was stuck, its front lodged in the sandbanks and the back half tilted across the canal. The year 2020 had already exposed the vulnerability of global supply chains as demand for goods bumped up against the pandemic's impact on manufacturing and distribution capabilities. The closure of the Suez Canal, many feared, was going to have serious consequences: a single ship had cut off the only lane for 12 percent of the world's trade. The capacity to move energy, automobile goods, household needs, and luxury items was going to take a huge hit. But it didn't.[12] Later supply-chain disruptions at the end of 2021 and the beginning of 2022 can be blamed on global economics and the pandemic but not on the *Ever Given*.

The closure of the Suez was a reminder of why it had originally been built in 1859. Virtually every container ship making the journey from the factories of Asia to the affluent consumer markets of Europe passes through the channel. So do large tankers laden with oil and natural gas. When *Ever Given* got stuck, nearly two hundred ships were waiting to get into the canal on either side; more were approaching.[13]

There weren't many options. But there was some guidance. There had been planning for the worst-case scenario because of security threats and environmental challenges in the Suez area for decades. Companies had viewed some of these near misses and had drawn up plans for mitigating the harm. They had every rational reason to believe the Suez was vulnerable. From 1967 to 1975, for example, the Suez Canal had closed due to the Six-Day War, and it did not open until after the Yom Kippur War.[14] Israel took control of the eastern bank of the canal; Egypt was on the western side. During those years, fourteen ships were trapped in a part of the canal called, ironically, the Great Bitter Lake. They came to

A failed attempt to release the *Ever Given* from Suez Canal. Source: Suez Canal Transit Authority.

be known as the Yellow Fleet. They tied themselves together and set up a micronation of sorts with designated ships for fancy dinners, music, and even a church. So for commerce to continue, ships moved to transit around the Cape of Good Hope, the southern tip of South Africa. It wasn't easy. The pivot added mileage, time, and energy needs for the ships and increased vulnerabilities due to wave currents.

In 2021, when the *Ever Given* blocked the route, it was not clear how long the Suez Canal would be closed. The viral images of a very small bulldozer trying to move sand to dislodge a much bigger boat seemed to suggest that the wait could be a while. It ended up being just a week, but the companies had done worst-case scenario planning. Time is of the essence with nearly ten billion in products transiting Suez every day, some of them perishables. Though the Cape of Good Hope adds weeks to the journey, even after Suez might open, companies knew that there would still be a backlog. The longer journey also meant shippers would spend more money on fuel consumption; navigational resistance due to bigger waves also increases fuel use and, unfortunately, carbon emissions. The Southern Ocean is a wild ride, and safety issues would also come into play. This is what happened with the 1967 closure, when the larger waves resulted in numerous safety incidents. The Cape of Good Hope is called the Graveyard of Ships for a reason.

The near misses in the recent past, and the long closure in 1967, motivated companies in the "just in time" supply chain to plan out contingencies should something actually shut the Suez Canal down. They really didn't have to predict the *Ever Given*. Who could? But the contingency planning, motivated by the near misses, provided the metrics to determine whether they would take the leap to Good Hope: time, cost, safety.[15] Companies made different calculations, but there was enough variety of response that there was an almost insignificant global impact with the canal being closed for a week. As hundreds of ships got stuck, major shipping giants like Maersk, Mediterranean Shipping, and Hapag-Lloyd started to move toward Africa. They had a plan. And we barely felt it downstream of the supply chain.

26.2

On April 15, 2013, Boston held its famous marathon. It was the target of a terror attack. The response was, as these things go, relatively successful. An Incident Command Structure (ICS) was utilized. First responders and police from across the Commonwealth were deployed to assist and worked their appropriate roles within the framework. Hospitals were prepped, also under an incident commander directing them, for the arrival of injured patients. Three people died at the finish line, but hundreds taken to area hospitals did not. Indeed, because of extensive planning for triage, not a single person who made it to a hospital died. The consequences were minimized; it was awful but not as bad as it might have been. It was a victory of sorts.

I had previously been the Commonwealth of Massachusetts's homeland security advisor to the governor. As we prepared for each year's marathon, and tested the ICS that would cover multiple jurisdictions along the marathon's route, we studied past near misses—an unanticipated storm, heat that gets too excessive so that the race might have to be called off—to answer a really complicated question: If there was no finish line, how could we get families back together?

I know this sounds like a nitpicky detail. Eventually, people will find each other. But it is a really basic desire during a crisis. There is increased panic if people can't find family members. If families are reunited, then some of the pressure and demands on first responders are eased. So an alternative finish line was part of planning efforts, a diversion to a few blocks away on Commonwealth Avenue. When the bombs went off, two police officers were first deployed to stand in the street and redirect runners.

Remember, these decisions were being made without knowing what had actually occurred at the finish line. Soon, it became clear that there wasn't going to be a finish whatsoever. The new goal was to reunite runners with their families and get them out as quickly as possible. "This more drastic measure which we took just after a few minutes was to shut down and go home. In other words, you can't come down here, the race is over, go away, go back, go home, go away. We didn't have a place to send them because we didn't know what was safe at that point," the Boston police commissioner at the time, Ed Davis, would tell me later.[16]

Thousands of runners were still approaching the finish line, an area that had been traumatically disrupted. Their families were often on the other side of that line. With cell service—assuming runners had access to their phones—under stress and not reliable, the question about how to unify the families, give them peace, and get them away from the tragedy was paramount.

But how? "There were times before when we thought we would have to close the marathon down. So we took what we learned for that and put it on steroids. In some ways it was just adrenaline, natural," Davis explained.[17] Davis doesn't remember who made the call to activate these backup plans, but the police set up a command post at an old armory nearby and used what they had—phones, social media, signage—to tell people to reunite at the cleared Boston Common. "We had never had to shut down the marathon before. But we had come close. That was enough to get us thinking about it."[18] It took no time, and reunification was completed swiftly. Get the runners and families together quickly and get them away. It was a victory of sorts.

THAT WAS CLOSE

If we know the miss will eventually happen, that the devil will in fact return, then we must take advantage of the time the near miss affords us. It should motivate us. It then can provide ample leeway, evidence, and planning on how best to respond when the disaster occurs. Jet-Blue, as described earlier, did not heed this advice. When it came to the weather, it didn't like to cancel; it pushed its pilots to the extremes—demanding they get to the front of the runway line so that once it was cleared, JetBlue would be first. It worked, JetBlue thought. Every near miss, every storm that came with a whimper and not a bang, every delay dealt with by passing out free cookies and popcorn, managed to head off the crisis. It was leadership by brinkmanship. Until it wasn't.

"People are hardwired to misinterpret or ignore the warnings embedded in these failures, and so they often go unexamined or, perversely, are seen as signs that systems are resilient and things are going well. Yet these seemingly innocuous events are often harbingers; if conditions shift slightly, or if luck does not intervene, a crisis erupts," scholars Catherine H. Tinsley, Robin L. Dillon, and Peter M. Madsen once wrote in their examination of catastrophes. Their studies on how to avert a catastrophe are illuminating.[19] They, too, accept the right side of the boom; their goal isn't prevention, it is to ward off a more devastating outcome. They urge institutions to use the near misses as an opportunity for worst-case-scenario planning. After all, since the disaster didn't happen, it affords a bit of luxury. Why squander it?

Think of Vaughan's "final disaster" warning that near misses are just a sign of an impending disaster, the final one. If we treat near misses as a sign the disaster will come rather than a sign that it can be averted, we won't feel much relief. Instead, we could avoid the normalization of deviance. It would force us to look at any planning, finances, and logistics that will be better positioned for when the near miss becomes real. Such an exercise can expose preparation and consequence management failures that ought to be fixed.

The basic response plan, such as activating ICS, can be made better through "what if" practice and training. This gives a company or institution the capacity to look ahead, to imagine that the crisis wasn't averted. It requires long-term thinking rather than efforts just to muster through. For example, during the COVID-19 pandemic, some restaurants survived, while so many faltered. The survivors were generally those that envisioned a different business model—takeout and delivery—and quickly shifted to capture homebound patrons' desire not to cook as much. They didn't view each night of the pandemic as some temporary inconvenience. Making it through one day didn't mean the problem was solved.

The financial world, again, provides an interesting analogy. In studying what advantages companies have when put under financial distress, the notion of the *uncertainty advantage* is dominant. This describes those companies that have the "right data, processes, commitment, and mindset" to anticipate volatility earlier and spring back faster.[20] They understand the importance of situational awareness. Disaster management like this is more of an interpretive dance than a fixed routine. So much is uncertain. There is still a rhythm and motion and lessons learned and protocols adopted, but they aren't fixed. The advantage goes to those who hear the music early and plan for it. Words like *agility* and *attentiveness* are often used, but preparing a workforce or a community for such an eventuality is of primary importance. This can be done by taking the initiative when it seems, for just a short while, that the disaster was averted and understanding it will return.

THE CHARMIN CRISIS

The toilet paper industry, as with most other major commodities, always had a very predictable market. Toilet paper is made, shipped, and sold. There isn't much backup because there doesn't need to be. Until the pandemic, demand and supply were relatively consistent. People bought toilet paper when they needed it, and it was manufactured around that need. It was, in supply-chain terms, a lean system. But when people went inside and were told to hunker down for months, demand calculations changed.

Initially, the industry wasn't ready.[21] They thought everything would always stay the same. Arist Mastorides, president of the Family Care Unit of consumer goods giant Kimberly-Clark, with brands like Cottonelle and Scott, headed home on the last day he was at the office in March 2020 after the CEO called an emergency meeting. He had heard that consumers were hoarding and wanted to see firsthand, so he stopped at his local Walmart near Lake Winnebago in Wisconsin. The shelves were empty. Mastorides was stunned. "A long gondola shelf that's completely empty of bathroom and facial tissue, I never in my life thought I would ever see that. That's a very unsettling thing."

A colleague in the same industry agreed. "We are prepared for thousands of different events, from cybersecurity attacks to earthquakes to fire," Julio Nemeth, the head of supply for P&G, also told *Fortune* magazine. "But we were not prepared for all of those happening at the same time, which is what the pandemic brought to us."[22]

Those earlier, discrete pressures were a prelude, however, to the real final disaster: a total disruption of the demand side of the equation brought on by the pandemic. These near misses taught the company how to respond. The intense pressure on the supply chain—the "Charmin crisis"—had to be addressed immediately in light of the uncertain toll the pandemic was likely to take and how long it was likely to last. Purchasing patterns were irrational and unpredictable. Companies began to shift accordingly based on their worst-case-scenario planning. Moving from a predictable demand operational setting, companies in essential goods reevaluated for a much more volatile, and yearlong, effort. "That includes fast-tracking onboarding for new suppliers, adding distribution sites, and using data to generate earlier demand-shock warnings."[23] These real-time adjustments were essential to eventually minimize the harm.

It is easy to get comfortable with routine, especially if a near miss was avoided. But the next disaster, and the one after that, will not look the same as the one we've been preparing for. Set the conditions of success—stop the harm, minimize the consequences—and the dance can take shape in real time with practice, training, and adaptability. The near misses are blessings. We must respond to them, and learn from them, so we are ready when the devil inevitably finds its target.

And the devil always will. You are here.

CHAPTER EIGHT

LISTEN TO THE DEAD

Beware of the Great Tsunami

In Japan, they call it 3.11, the day in March 2011 when a three-part disaster resulted in a catastrophe of biblical proportions. The epicenter of the 9.0–9.1 Richter scale earthquake was the undersea east of the Oshika Peninsula off Japan. It lasted six minutes and remains the fourth-most powerful earthquake ever recorded in the world. That earthquake triggered tsunami waves of up to 130 feet. As described earlier, those waves then caused a meltdown at the Fukushima Daiichi nuclear facility. The loss of electrical power then shut off the cooling systems, leading to hydrogen gas accumulation. As workers tried to cool the facility manually—using water from fire trucks—that process of venting led to the expulsion of radioactive material into the atmosphere and groundwater. About thirty thousand people were killed on 3.11. Most perished from the tsunami and the waters. To this day, Fukushima is still uninhabitable.

Listen to your elders. High above in the mountains on the edge of Aneyoshi, a tiny coastal village not far from Fukushima, warnings are carved into the rock. It is a message from the nineteenth-century survivors of large tsunamis. Its inscription reads: "High dwellings are the peace and harmony of our descendants. Remember the calamity of the great tsunamis. Do not build homes

A nineteenth-century tsunami warning in Japan. *Smithsonian Magazine.*

below this point."[1] But they built. The stones remain, but the population does not.

The reasons for the neglected warnings are complicated and relate to Japan's history, politics, and energy supply needs. After all, it is more likely than not that an ocean earthquake will lead to a tsunami. The consequences of that were totally knowable, including damage to the nuclear plant and total loss of power. Still, reactors were built on fault lines and below tsunami levels. A variety of studies tried to figure out how things got so bad. It had to do with how the entire system of the nuclear industry was built after World War II.

Japan is the only nation to date that has suffered a nuclear attack; the 1945 bombings of Nagasaki and Hiroshima have, obviously, a lasting impact. That meant that when Japan needed to rely on nuclear power for its energy needs, the public was wary, to say the least. According to Akihisa Shiozaki, a lawyer who organized an independent investigation of the nuclear disaster, the country was sold a myth: "the absolute safeness" of nuclear power.[2] As more and more plants were built, the symbiotic structure of industry and government aligned around the necessity of nuclear power. Local opposition had to be managed, which meant not talking about the potential for a worst-case scenario. The stone's warning about the "calamity of the great tsunamis" was ignored. "Well, that myth of absolute safeness developed over the years into a culture where it almost became taboo to even talk about this. . . . Discussing a worst-case scenario was feared because it might bring panic to the citizens. And therefore, it was omitted from the regulatory discussions," said Shiozaki.[3]

Disregarding history harmed Japan in two distinct ways. First, the nation rejected the messages from its ancestors. Second, World War II's legacy gave leaders a perverse incentive to delude the public into a dangerous sense of security. Of course, nuclear power is inherently dangerous. Many nations live with that risk. But few believe in its "absolute safeness." A report commissioned by the legislative branch, the National Diet of Japan, concluded with the overwhelming assessment, "The government, the regulators, TEPCO (the nuclear energy company) management, and the Kantei (prime minister's office) lacked the preparation and the mindset to efficiently operate an emergency response to an accident of this scope. None, therefore, were effective in preventing or limiting the consequential damage."[4] Japan could have better anticipated, and tried to mitigate, the losses after an earthquake and tsunami. The dominance of the nuclear industry in Japan created a narrative of industrial invincibility, immune from the real lessons the ancestors left behind: "Do not build homes below this point."

But they did.

HOW WE DIE

That people die in a crisis is, unfortunately, a given. Things break, institutions falter, societies buckle under the stress. The mistakes made may or may not be easily remedied, but there will be mistakes. A perfectly managed crisis is an oxymoron; if perfectly handled, it is not really a crisis. After the bodies are identified, or the debris picked up, or the systems put back into place, there is a tendency—maybe natural—to move on. Fix this. Tinker with that. And a horrible experience is best remembered, often, by not remembering at all.

Many major disasters or events have some sort of commission or blue-ribbon group to determine what went wrong and what might be learned to prepare for the future. They can be thorough and help expose facts and lessons, such as the 9/11 Commission, whose historic words—"a failure of imagination"—captured the world's attention. In so many cases, the reasons for the disaster—the left-of-boom elements—are easy to come by: levees broke, intelligence dots weren't connected, a network was vulnerable, a virus wasn't contained early enough. Fixes are urged to ensure that an identical catastrophe doesn't happen again. Who could be against that? But a thorough review has an additional purpose in an era of disasters: it not only confirms that people have died, but it can expose *how* people died. There is a difference.

In the 2020 hurricane season, there were thirty named storms, more than ever before. Storms were so plentiful that the National Hurricane Center (NHC) had to turn to the Greek alphabet—alpha, beta, and so on—once it had passed Z. Twelve of those storms made land in the US, another new record. Hurricane Laura in Louisiana would prove to be the biggest, creating seventeen-foot storm surges, the highest ever recorded. The NHC launched a massive messaging campaign throughout in an effort that minimized fatalities, using the dramatic word *unsurvivable* to impress upon people how serious Laura could be.

There was not one fatality because of the surge or hurricane. But still, twenty-eight people died, most of these after the storm had passed. It wasn't the waters. It was the gas. As the storm devastated the electrical grid, many communities had to rely on emergency generators;

various areas in Southwest Louisiana had no access to power for weeks. Those generators proved to be unsafe for many. The majority of the deaths were in fact people dying from carbon monoxide poisoning rather than from the storm itself.[5]

These are stupid deaths, often called indirect deaths. As hurricane forecasting has improved, information has helped make us safer and better prepared for surging waters. In turn, fewer people die from direct causes, such as flooding and high winds, yet people are still dying. These indirect causes include heart attacks, car accidents, electrocution, and carbon monoxide.

We've similarly learned about blizzards in the last few decades. It turns out most people do not die from the snow or cold. They mostly die from carbon monoxide poisoning as well, more often than not in their cars. In the 1978 blizzard in New England, nearly one hundred people died during a surprise storm, one that came in so fast it was almost impossible to prepare for. Once the snow started falling, people got into their cars to rush home or check in on family members. Soon many got stuck. Without help on the horizon, while freezing, people kept their car engines on as the exhaust pipe froze as well. Carbon monoxide would ultimately kill seventy-two of them.[6]

This is why today, governors throughout New England and in colder climates regularly institute travel bans well before the snow starts. If they wait too long, the disaster will kill in ways having nothing to do directly with snow. A goal is certainly to protect first responders and keep streets open to plow. But mostly it is to keep people from dying of carbon monoxide poisoning. It is the immediate aftermath period that can prove deadliest, when people turn to makeshift processes—generators barely used, fireplaces not cleaned out—and die. There is an irony here; as our systems of response become more and more sophisticated for recurring disasters, and people take heed of familiar threats, the disaster can still be challenging and lethal. How people die matters.

WHAT WE ONCE KNEW

I've emphasized that historical patterns, although helpful, cannot always serve as guides for what we might anticipate in the future. The threats are changing too quickly and occurring too rapidly. But that is not to say there is no role for history to promote better response and consequence management purposes. One obvious reason is because stupid, or indirect, deaths can always be avoided. Another reason, though, is that we often learn the wrong lessons from these disasters. We make the wrong assumptions, like water or wind being the cause of hurricane deaths. These initial assumptions about what occurred, and therefore how to fix it, will change over time. We must accurately memorialize how people die.

This happened with later studies of the mass shooting at Colorado's Columbine High School on April 20, 1999. We believe a story about the two student murderers, Eric Harris and Dylan Klebold, that has not held up to examination: they were not misfits and goth advocates who lived in a dark world. All of that was a myth. They were well-adapted boys, beloved, who did something horrible.[7] And as the events of that day were reviewed, it also became clear that the protocols for how to deal with active shooters had to change.

As the two student killers walked the hallways shooting, students were told to hide in the school's library. The problem was that nothing protected them there. One after another, the killers targeted the captive students. After the massacre, twelve students and one teacher had lost their lives; the shooters committed suicide. In subsequent years, as more was learned about that day, it was clear that the students died because they were unable to escape from the library. And so those who began to help schools deal with the truly horrific American phenomenon of school shootings began to promote the concept of "run, hide, fight." Run first if you can. Get out of harm's way. Who died and didn't die in that high school wasn't merely a matter of luck;

it was a question of location. An important lesson from the tragedy of Columbine is that we taught our children to run.

As a mother, I found these school shootings devastating. With decades of mass shootings, we've now learned that there is no benefit for first responders to delay entry into a facility. Previously, they had assumed that a shooter had some agenda and that by not entering, police could convince them to stop their violence. After Columbine, police were trained in a new tactic: *immediate action rapid deployment.*[8] Speed, in other words, could have saved those children. It is worth noting that years later, conventional wisdom has begun to change again. The new understanding is that students could know what to do if there was an active shooter if it was explained to them but that formal active shooter drills are less beneficial than once thought. The trauma to students, especially younger ones, outweighs any benefit they may gain.[9]

In design and planning, the same is true. Bridges falling are headlines. It is a tragedy. But we must return to the site to determine how, in fact, it fell. On November 7, 1940, the Tacoma Narrows Bridge, the third-largest suspension bridge in the world, collapsed. The bridge connected Tacoma to the Kitsap Peninsula in Puget Sound and had opened just a few months earlier. It was a spectacular bridge failure, a technological wonder that didn't last a year.

What brought the bridge down was wind. It was not just any wind, though, or the wind that examiners originally believed brought the bridge down. For some time, engineers believed the collapse was due to something called resonant frequency. Resonant frequency describes how much an object can absorb vibrational energy. Too much resonant frequency, too much pressure on the system unable to absorb it, and catastrophe follows. It was assumed that the wind moved the bridge naturally at first, but then pushed the frequency too hard, too strong, for too long, and it couldn't sustain the pressure.

That simple assumption proved incorrect. Decades later, science would later change the narrative.[10] When an object is suspended between two points, it is built to move to absorb impacts such as wind. The capacity to vibrate is built in, and we know how to build bridges to do so. That November 1940 day, the wind was so strong and continual that it caused something new, a *flutter*. The flutter served as an extra push at the ends of the suspended object, causing them to move perpendicular to the wind (rather than with the wind). Airplane manufacturers have learned to account for flutter in the design of a plane's wings. But no engineer thought it could happen on a bridge. With the unique intense wind, the flutter was uncontrolled, twisting back and forth, breaking a steel suspension cable. The bridge could just not hold.

Fixing resonant frequency is a very different effort than addressing flutter in a suspension bridge. The latter requires buttressing end posts. Without such knowledge, bridges would continue to be built without a focus on flutter. Modern science led to a new engineering subfield called bridge aerodynamics and aeroelasticity. It pushed engineers to monitor new bridges as well that might be prone to flutter-like damage, including London's Millennium Bridge and Russia's Volgograd Bridge.[11] Both of these major bridges had delayed openings and abrupt closings due to concerns over flutter.

Any review of what went wrong or how we can do better has to begin with the fundamentals, not the results. Take Facebook, for example, if we must. Mark Zuckerberg created a product, not just a platform. It connected people, he told us. He let us share memories and pictures, reacquaint ourselves, and meet strangers. Life would be better because we would be together. Facebook was sold as a benign company with a leader who seemed young enough to avoid judgment. But then reality hit the company: it had to monetize all the fun. So it turned to an advertising-based model, where we—Facebook's users—actually became the product. Our information and our desires were targeted by the company for sale; advertisers would use that data to focus their efforts.[12]

Zuckerberg was the perfect salesperson for the pitch. And he told regulators and legislators, privacy advocates, and those who would want to protect democracy not to worry about his growing power to control what we knew. By 2016, most Americans were absorbing their news through Facebook; it was no longer a platform but a publisher. The "news" became a sold commodity, targeted to those who would want to read it. Whether it was true or not was not Facebook's worry.[13]

As complaints grew about all the disinformation, Zuckerberg defended himself by what seemed a completely rational explanation. We wouldn't want him to have the power to decide what is true, he would argue to congressional investigators and reporters. For Facebook to be the adjudicator of truth, the CEO claimed, was worse than letting information flow, even if some of it was false. The explanation sounded pretty solid.

Over time, it was clear that the argument was a total self-serving manipulation. He was playing with our assumptions about information. By claiming he didn't want such authority to decide the truth, he was hiding the fact that he had already asserted considerable authority. His decision not to decide was a value-laden decision itself. It was favoring treachery; it let the misinformation and disinformation flourish. Zuckerberg was claiming he was agnostic. He was instead running the devil's errands.

Facebook would spend a large chunk of its efforts post-2016 defending its business model, one that was flawed by design. It would promise to get better; piecemeal efforts, including the creation of a "Supreme Court" to independently assess questions of truth and usage, were created. It has not changed, though it apologizes a lot. It will not learn because it refuses to look at the primary, fundamental, even existential decision it had made—deciding not to decide.[14] It will repeat history because it has no interest in learning from it.

THE LESSONS ARE WRITTEN ON THE HEADSTONES

In a world where we no longer treat disasters as random and rare, the necessity to learn quickly and honestly from the disaster is all the more pressing. Disasters are also teachers, educating us on what we can do better next time. But those lessons should be captured in a meaningful, open way. Otherwise, the real lessons will decay.

On September 29, 1915, a hurricane landed in New Orleans, Louisiana. It was an unnamed massive hurricane, one that would kill 275 people. Houses were destroyed, whole areas washed away, and the Saint Louis Cathedral sustained damage. The city was thrilled even to have survived. As city planners assessed the damage that lay before them, they drew one basic lesson: the new levees built to protect the city were just fine. The city could and should grow.[15] And so it did.

Andy Horowitz, a Tulane assistant professor who specializes in urban and environmental history, is the author of *Katrina: A History, 1915–2015*. Horowitz forcefully argues that it was those lessons from 1915 that set the stage for the Katrina disaster in 2005. The city learned all the wrong ones, he told me. City leaders' celebratory tone became an excuse for growth, and New Orleans would be dubbed "the City That Care Forgot." Sounds like fun, but the name also is ominous. Instead of viewing the disaster as a moment in time, Horowitz insists that disasters reflect the decisions made well before the event itself.[16] Learning the wrong lessons can lead to massive harm. We cannot avoid hurricanes, but we can avoid some of their most dire consequences by learning from the hurricane before and preparing better. Horowitz urges disaster managers to remember that Katrina is just a name. What happened to New Orleans was the result of thousands of public policy decisions made decades before.

"The New Orleans Sewerage and Water Board," Horowitz writes in the introduction to the book, "the agency charged with protecting the city from floods, concluded that its new drainage system had passed a defining test." It was a dangerous lesson; new neighborhoods developed after were the most harmed by Katrina. "Tracing the outline of the Katrina flood reveals the shape of New Orleans as it stood nine decades earlier: most houses built before 1915 did not flood, but most houses built after the Sewerage and Water Board's 1915 call for further growth did."[17]

This seems counterintuitive, but it is correct. New Orleans's older areas, and its homes, survived Katrina because they had survived the 1915 flood. When the city opened its doors to further growth, despite the fact it was built below shoreline, the newer areas could not withstand the next big event. There was no reason to believe that they would have survived 1915 because the areas weren't populated then. Rather than the flashing red lights that warned that in fact the city could not sustain growth, planners looked in the wrong direction and took their lessons from what survived on the dry side. When Katrina came, emergency managers had too much confidence in the levees, unprepared for the flooding that would occur, because even if they should falter, nothing bad had happened the last time in 1915. That erroneous lesson was a fundamental reason thousands died when Katrina hit.

THE SEVENTH WAVE

After every disaster or crisis, it is imperative for us to take a deep, hard look at what occurred. That review must be continuous over time. In the previous chapter, I highlighted the need for mechanisms to help us pivot so we aren't tied to formal planning or responses. Here, I urge that when the response is done, we need to constantly revisit the event in the days, months, and even years to come and understand what we can do to better minimize the consequences. Of course, given how disasters work now, these reviews will be occurring as new disasters arrive. Consider it a constant feedback loop, then.

What is essential is that we view these reviews as more than about root causes or systemic challenges. That people died is no mystery by the time the crisis is over. But a new crisis is surely to come, and those root causes will take a while to solve. Instead, the tactical and operational decisions made at the moment of boom, and the assumptions they were based on, always have to be challenged. Why, after all, were those kids at Columbine told to run to the library?

Emergency managers often perform "hot washes" immediately after a crisis. It is exactly as it sounds. It is intended to be a scorching performance review of what went wrong and right. They are helpful because memories have not faded yet. But they capture the heat of the moment. These after-action reviews (AAR) are documented in a lessons learned review and, if done right, help guide future training. Public and private institutions are used to performing these postmortems in order to do better next time. These reports are done after the event, assess blame and accountability, and provide recommendations for the future. But they only capture what we believe to be true at the time. As years and decades pass, those lessons can change or be forgotten. We must keep returning to the past disasters so we can be prepared for all the future ones.

The 2004 Indian Ocean tsunami killed 250,000 people. Another 150,000 died from diseases or deprivations related to the tsunami and the struggling response in the days and weeks after. Stupid deaths. The energy, eventually released through the waves, from when the Indian continental plate crashed under the Burma plate had the impact of 1,500 Hiroshima nuclear bombs.[18] For someone not familiar with tsunamis, like me, determining who died would seem so simple: if you were close to the water as the tsunami formed, you perished, and if you were farther away, you didn't. Yes, the tsunami resulted in a lot of deaths not related to the water—disease and lack of clean water would later kill many more—but in that moment of impact, survival seemed just a matter of geography.

But that assessment is not accurate. Where you were during the moment of impact matters, but so does memory. Tsunamis, massive tsunamis, are not unique to that area, though they are rare. It turns out that historic tsunamis had taught many close to the waters what to do to protect themselves. The problem was that those lessons had decayed over time or were not shared. Too many victims were unaware of them; new government leaders had better things to do than worry about a rare event. When the tsunami started to form and suck the water out from the ocean, exposing the shoreline and serving as a curiosity rather than an omen, not enough people knew the lessons from past tsunamis: when the waters recede fast, run for the hills.

In 2004, the populations of whole villages were saved not because they were lucky but because the memory of the 1907 tsunami had been shared from generation to generation: when the earth moves, so will the oceans. That lesson was told, year after year, to those who understood that the oceans would move again.[19] So it was no surprise that more recently built villages, with new immigrants, or places that housed tourists, like hotels, were completely eviscerated in 2004. Residents or visitors had no historical sense of what was to come as the ocean tides pulled back, feeding a massive wave forming that would kill in no time.

When the waters recede, run for the hills. The sea nomads of Thailand knew this.[20] These are members of the Moken tribe who have lived on the Thai islands for centuries. On that December 26 morning, tribal members noticed the waters were too still. There was no wind; dolphins were swimming out to deeper waters; deep sea fish seemed to be appearing close to shore. They started to evacuate quickly. The tribe's chief, Salama, started shouting to tribal members and tourists as loud as he could: "This is laboon, an ancient thing that has swallowed whole islands before." He had learned from his forefathers that laboon was known as the "seventh wave," the deadly one.[21]

There were no fancy reports or commissions after the 1907 tsunami. No congressional hearings or lessons learned. Instead, there was an oral history of laboon, passed on through the generations. These oral histories, throughout disaster management, often explain why indigenous populations do better when disaster strikes. Visitors and new immigrants would see the ocean depleted and might think it was interesting or curious. They had no idea of the danger of the seventh wave.

But the story doesn't end there, fortunately. Because in a world where there will be more tsunamis, the many countries of the Indian Ocean began to prepare for the next one. After 2004, they established protocols and education campaigns and sought to engage civic society in consequence management, utilizing new tools and techniques in the hopes that as many people as possible would know to run for the hills if the waters disappear. Would it work? The problem is that to actually know, government authorities would probably have to wait for the next tsunami. That next test would provide evidence of success or failure.

As described throughout this book, a fundamental tenet of consequence management is that systems to protect the public need to be practiced and validated. This is a greater imperative in an era of catastrophes. "This is a test, this is only a test" are familiar words, after all. First responders do constantly test their response plans. These efforts can be small tabletop exercises or large simulations of catastrophic events with people acting the parts of victims. Some of these exercises are helpful; others are a waste of time. But in the end, they don't fully suffice because everybody knows it is just a test. There is no double-blind evaluation in which both the responders and the potential victims are uncertain if it's simulated or real. Without such a test, the actors aren't necessarily following their instincts; they're following the script.

Most scholars in disaster management acknowledge that the truest evaluation of any response system is one that gets as close to a catastrophe as real life allows but falls short of real damage. A near miss, essentially. What can we learn from a bad thing that didn't happen but that, for a brief while, everyone thought would? The best way to determine whether tsunami response efforts got better would be a situation when everybody thought a tsunami was coming.

Seven years after the 2004 tsunami, an earthquake struck the coast of Indonesia. There was no tsunami that time, but the Indonesians didn't know that at first. During the few hours in 2011 between fear and the all-clear, a real exercise took place. It showed that the lessons learned from 2004 were, for the most part, working. The changes Indonesia had put in place after 2004—to alert people that when the waters recede, run fast, so very fast—succeeded.

Updated monitoring from the US Geological Survey helped pinpoint where the Indonesian quake struck. Almost immediately, warning sirens turned on, many of them from local mosques—a brilliant placement of an alert system, given the mosques' central role and location in most villages. Because of extensive efforts by the Indonesian government and the United Nations, people were trained what to do, where to go, and what to bring. Hotels had extensive signage and information for guests in the event of another warning. When the sirens went off, people walked, drove, or biked away from identified risk areas. The evacuation wasn't flawless. Indonesia has admitted that its alert system, put in place after 2004, faltered in some places. Some evacuation routes got jammed as people traveled miles away, not knowing when the water might strike.

The response systems after 2004 were not perfect when they were tested in 2011, but they were better than before. And, likely, better for the next tsunami and the ones after that.

And so on. And so forth. You are here.

WHERE TO BEGIN IF IT NEVER ENDS

Richter's Demise

I grew up in Los Angeles, California. I say this because a not insignificant part of my upbringing involved some discussion, preparation, or response to an earthquake or the threat of one. We didn't think much of it; it seemed just a part of the geography, a natural threat that every child understood and had drilled for. There were exercises in the classroom when teachers would—at some designated time unbeknownst to us—yell, "Earthquake!" and we would drop to the floor, under our desks, or in the doorways if we were in the gym or outside. Our house was designed for what we viewed as inevitable: we bolted armoires and speakers to the walls, we learned how to turn off the gas, and we had lists of phone numbers and contingency plans to communicate if the landlines went out.

We also came to understand and adapt to the way scientists measure earthquakes. We lived, and possibly died, by the Richter scale. The scale was named after the Caltech seismologist Charles Richter, who in 1935 invented a mathematical formula that compared seismic waves to determine the strength of the earth shifts. People who lived in earthquake-prone areas came to intuit Richter's scale: Anything under 4.0 was a joke. Quakes in the 4.0–5.0 range meant that the slight jolt we felt in the middle of the night was in fact what we expected. When an earthquake was above 5.0, we knew to expect damage and may have even freaked out a little. Close to 6.0 or above? That was real. Perhaps our parents yelled at us to get under the bed or run into our rooms to make sure we were fine. We were likely to hear about significant damage, possibly even deaths. Richter was a warning and a companion.

I left California when I was eighteen and have not lived there since. The fear of earthquakes was replaced by hurricane season, blizzards, and the growing sense in Boston that the sea we had built around was rising. When I heard about earthquakes, I got worried because my parents were still in California and laughed when a small New England tremor—maybe a 3.5—resulted in a flurry of news alerts and weeks-long discussion. "When I was young, we didn't even bother to wake up if it wasn't above five point zero on the Richter," I would say cockily to my kids, who were not used to the earth moving.

So I could be forgiven for missing a significant shift in earthquake calculations. The Richter scale no longer exists. By the 1990s, its cold calculation of impact was seen as scientifically inaccurate. It wasn't reliable for bigger quakes, those above 8.0. More importantly, it was based on instruments that worked best when close to the faults, within one hundred miles or so. That was great for Southern California, where Richter lived and worked, but not so great for other parts of the world. So over time, without much fanfare, scientists created better, more accurate ways to measure the magnitude of quakes. "You can rank people by health, by intelligence, by beauty, by weight," Paul Richards, a Columbia University seismologist, remarked about the scale's demise. "And you can do the same thing with earthquakes."[1]

Today, we use a calculation known as the *moment magnitude*. Moment magnitude measures how much the earth moves and the size of the fault; if both are big, the moment magnitude increases. While the inputs into the new system were different, those numbers were then adjusted to conform to the Richter scale because so many people had come to rely on it. Thus, while scientists and seismologists altered the very way that we measure the earth's movements, they did so in a way that the public could comprehend. It reminds us that the way we think about, structure, and communicate harm is always changing. We may not know it, or even care, but whole systems are abandoned and reimagined without much drama.

The way we consider success must also change. There is nothing fatalistic in this realization. Crisis management must now face a new scale, the *less bad* one. Successive disasters create the necessity to consider our specialized responses as not so specialized anymore. Disasters become democratic. But recurring harm is also an opportunity for us to get better each time. This book has been an effort to similarly reinvent the Richter scale for disasters. It has begged for a shift to a calculation of success that is measured by a metric of *less bad*. This narrative accepts harm as well as fights it. While the details of each step may take some time to understand and implement, everyone—corporate and education leaders, small business owners and city managers, global institutions, and families—can begin today without much fanfare. You are here.

THE DAY AFTER TOMORROW

The year is 1999. While drilling for ice samples in Antarctica, Jack Hall, an American paleoclimatologist, notices the ice shelf beginning to split into pieces. As massive ocean temperatures drop, he concludes that there is a coming ice age. He keeps trying to warn people, but few will listen. Millions perish as storms sweep across the globe, which eventually plunges into cold. Art Bell and Whitley Strieber's book *The Coming Global Superstorm* served as the basis for the blockbuster film *The Day After Tomorrow*, starring Dennis Quaid and Jake Gyllenhaal.[2] Throughout the movie, scientists monitoring the earth's shift try to warn political leaders of the inevitable, but to no avail. There is always tomorrow.

Day One is today. And it begins with a baseline assessment. Everyone has the capacity to start on the right side of the boom by not being wary of initiating it in the first place. Where to actually begin—because you will never end—may take some easing into. Three basic baseline questions can help: Where is the money? Where are the people? Where are you?

First: the money. Money and budgets are a reflection of priorities. A good intention needs money to back it up. There are two buckets to look at immediately. The first is the overall allocation of a budget that goes into security and safety efforts. There is no perfect number: 50 percent seems too high; 2 percent may be too low. A rough guess about home improvements or repairs to address potential vulnerabilities, redundancies, and security systems can provide some transparency. These efforts give a baseline sense of how seriously, or not, we take security and preparedness efforts. It is just a number. It will be clear if that number is not defensible when you imagine defending it to shareholders, the media, or your spouse after an event. Is it something you could live with and explain?

That is not the only number to take into account. I often ask students to consider spending "one hundred pennies" across security investments.

I use this analogy in class to get students to think about how, depending on the threat, they would spend their money on either the

Allocation of security money.

left or right side of the boom. Let's say that as you look carefully at your budget, it turns out that the institution is spending eighty pennies on left-of-boom investments compared to twenty pennies on right-of-boom investments. Nuclear facilities want to spend significant amounts on protecting themselves from a disaster. But do those remaining twenty pennies provide enough resources to prepare for when the facility may be the focus of a boom?

This simple reckoning is an exercise that costs nothing but can reveal much. It can expose where a company or organization has placed value (how much they spend on security) and the priorities within that investment (left or right of boom). It doesn't take detailed accounting, only the back-of-envelope type of effort, but it will be illuminating. It may provide solace, but more likely than not, it will expose glaring and indefensible gaps. Those gaps can eventually be addressed, but first you need to know where they are in order to do better.

Second: the architecture. As described throughout, good policies follow good bones. Place matters. An institution creates offices and departments, all with their reporting structures, and some may not make sense. Small businesses might find that too much is dependent on a part-time consultant or a work-from-home employee. If there isn't an organizational chart now, then make one, as it probably would be helpful for many reasons. At home, as I have found, all information residing in the memory capacity of a mother who is often on the road and who has a bad short-term memory isn't a great system. These reviews will show how prominent and unified the safety and security apparatus is. It will also show how not prominent and not unified it is. Are offices randomly placed that instead should be part of a unified effort? Are there free-floating personnel and responsibilities that seem to exist in some weird bubble with no oversight and little access to leadership? Did you forget a plan for the dog?

Much like a budget, an organizational chart will expose the indefensible or inexplicable. This chart, for example, was first released by

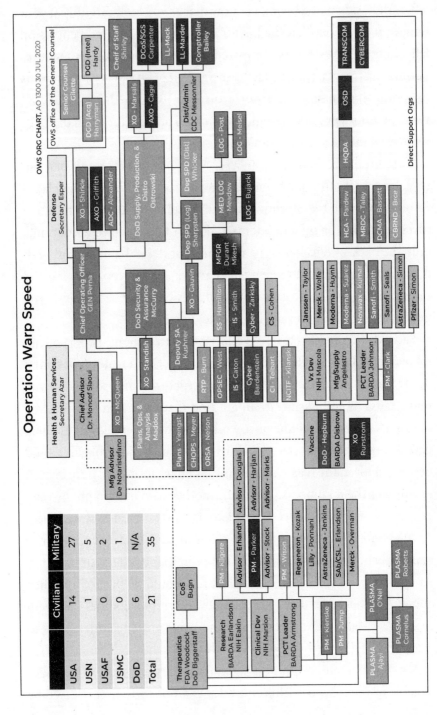

Operation Warp Speed

OWS ORG CHART, AO 1300 30 JUL 2020

OWS office of the General Counsel

	Civilian	Military
USA	14	27
USN	1	5
USAF	0	2
USMC	0	1
DoD	6	N/A
Total	**21**	**35**

Vaccine distribution plan draft, obtained by STAT News.

the Trump administration to explain its plan for the vaccination distribution efforts. It was part of Operation Warp Speed, the successful effort to create and manufacture a vaccine. The last part, delivery throughout the nation to be administered into people's arms, was first described in this draft chart.

It was just a marker, a way to indicate how they were thinking about delivering the vaccine throughout the country. As we now know, those efforts were difficult and slow at first. That was likely to happen regardless of the administration; most major distribution efforts start that way. But there were aspects of this that struck me as decisions that would be hard to explain and would likely result in a cluster of mismanagement.

I couldn't tell who was in charge. That's a problem. Who was calling the shots? It wasn't clear whether it was the Health and Human Services Department or the military. I'm all for unity of effort and whole-of-government approaches, but I also believe that someone has to be at the top eventually. Without a lead agency, who could be fired if it all failed? I'm not joking. To be in this field is to live with the expectation "that they will happily walk you to the guillotine," former Coast Guard commandant Thad Allen, once told me. This was advice on a very late night when we got wind that the White House might be inclined to do just that during the spill response efforts.

There is an additional aspect to the chart that made no sense to me. It placed a lot of responsibilities on the military for what was fundamentally a civilian effort. Our homeland and a lot of communities in our nation are not used to uniformed military in their midst. It is not how a public health campaign should work, as community members should feel comfortable in these spaces. John Auerbach, then the CEO of Trust for America's Health, noted the same when he remarked about the leaked vaccination plan to STAT news. "[Troops] don't know who the doctors are or where the community health centers are located or what resources they have. They don't know where the pharmacies are. Public health people do know."[3] A simple visual can help guide the eye to see where the pieces fit together or crowd each other out.

Third: the "I." This isn't about mindfulness or finding yourself. Throughout, the lessons from tragedies past provide essential guidance for all of us. A corporate CEO, a small business owner, and a parent all would benefit from some worst-case-scenario planning. The goal is for leaders, defined broadly, to assess how their own time, resources, and efforts are spent. Do months go by without them even touching base with the security team? When was the last briefing? Can they answer basic questions if asked randomly? Indeed, do they even know who runs the whole thing? ("That guy" isn't an adequate answer.) Have you checked the batteries in the closet? Did you ever get that generator? What about water? Do we have extra dog food?

I'll often ask CEOs or institutional leaders how often they meet with various members of their teams. I do this because time, like money, is a tell. They'll answer by saying they meet with the COO several times a day, the CFO at least a few times a week. They'll often admit that they try to avoid the general counsel. The communications and marketing teams are always at the ready. But as for the chief security officer, or equivalent, the answer is often some variation of this: "Well, he's former FBI, so he knows what he is doing." They tell me this without any idea of how dangerous that attitude can be or how it can have a significant impact on the whole institution. It is the wrong answer.

That emergency manager's refrain—be ready because you don't want to be passing out business cards at the scene of a disaster—is not a mantra exclusive to the operational or tactical teams. It really is remarkable how little the basics of response capacity are known to those who are ultimately in charge. Few CEOs keep their jobs after a major catastrophe: BP, Boeing, Sony, ERCOT. They all think they will. They don't. Given that termination is likely your destiny, I tell them, wouldn't you rather get fired after you helped save people? The answer is always yes.

I am well aware that the ability to prepare for disaster management is often the luxury of those with time and capacity. When people can barely make their monthly rent, it seems a little precious to discuss building bandwidth. The reason, however, why each of us should embrace the day before tomorrow is to relieve limited public safety and response resources for those who have less capacity to do so. We must recognize that, in this era of catastrophes, our preparedness allows for more help to flow to those who can't.

These three preliminary inquiries—money, architecture, and commitment—set the foundation for what needs to be done in anticipation of the disasters to come. These are knowable, sometimes complex, but always necessary.

Once these basic questions are asked, and answered, the process of preparing for the right side of the boom can begin. Every one of us can begin. Whether it is challenging the last line of defense myth or figuring out ways to stop the bleed, any of these efforts will help for consequence minimization for the days after today. We don't have to worry about probabilities of some risk assessment or the form the devil takes. At first, I wondered whether the steps laid out in the preceding chapters should be steps—as in, do this and then that. In reality, some are better than none, even though all is better than some. Each of these improvements can stand alone.

FINALLY, A WORD ON RESILIENCE

I have avoided using the term *resilience*. It is an important concept, essential for the times ahead, but its focus is on the investments in the future that can better protect us. The goal here is mostly on what we can do better in the moment of the boom rather than how to rebuild after. We know a more resilient society is one that can withstand the booms, over and over again, better and better each time. Levees will hold because the investment put into them means they will withstand the next storm. Encouraging resilience and resilience planning is the path forward for long-term capacity to withstand and adapt to the challenges and crises ahead.

This notion that dividends result from resiliency was best articulated by Judith Rodin, the former president of the Rockefeller Foundation, in her groundbreaking 2014 work for *The Resilience Dividend: Being Strong in a World Where Things Go Wrong*.[4] Rodin articulated two benefits for building resilience. First, it helps communities and businesses better withstand the disruption; it minimizes the impact. Second, a resiliency focus actually helps "to build new relationships, take on new endeavors and initiatives, and reach out for new opportunities, ones that may never have been imagined before. This is the resilience dividend."[5]

It is a hopeful, complementary message and one that will surely benefit us in the decades to come. But I fear that the focus on resiliency makes us only look ahead for the ultimate success. If everything is about resiliency, then nothing is about response. The investments that can make us stronger don't need to wait until the bodies are gone and the debris is picked up. The steps described here are focused on minimizing the impact of the boom so that—in that moment—some sort of success can be achieved even in the midst of horror. I never mean to minimize the importance of all these deep policy issues, but answering the question "What are we to do now at that moment of boom?" is often neglected by leaders and managers.

We just always seem to be looking for big fixes and forgetting that the present ones matter too. Our fascination with resiliency can force our focus too far into the future rather than on the sustained preparedness that can get us through today. In August 2021, the UN's Intergovernmental Panel on Climate Change (IPCC) released a report that sent people who care about its future, and climate change activists, into a spiral of doom.[6] They have every reason to feel that way. The advisory board wrote confidently that the temperatures are rising and that some effects of those changes are now irreversible. It was pretty confident in its views, basing its assessment on data and better modeling since its previous report in 2013. Everything is horrible, reporters and analysts said. It is too late![7]

It is never too late. The report was much more sophisticated than that. The IPCC first put into perspective the probability of some of the more extreme doomsday scenarios out there. With cold calculation, it bought us some time. This may not seem much solace, but it puts the outlier scenarios, the "tails" of scenario planning, in perspective. It gives us something to work with. The IPCC didn't stop there.

What was missing from any analysis was that the report also spoke of human agency right now. We are, in fact, on Day One, it warned us. And so we must embrace our ability to mitigate the consequences of the harms to come. We can get better at our response, with greater vigor, focus, and professionalism. The report was depressing, but not at all fatalistic. It is the first report of its kind that actually embraces the notion of consequence minimization as an imperative of the climate change agenda.[8]

"Sometimes climate change is treated like the sky is falling, which implies a final crash," said Peter Huybers, a professor of earth and planetary affairs at Harvard University.[9] He was clear that there is plenty to be anxious about, but he viewed the defeatism that permeated so much of the commentary around the report as self-defeating. The sky, in other words, is always falling. The imperative is what are we going to do now to protect ourselves. It isn't a matter of just carrying on.

Most of us are familiar with the slogan "Keep Calm and Carry On." It often appears on posters with the queen's crown, suggesting its influence in the efforts of public messaging campaigns during World War II as Britain was peppered by Nazi bombs. The slogan has its variants—"Keep Calm and Call Me Maybe" or "Keep Calm and Marathon," the latter an ode to Boston's response to the Boston Marathon bombings.

We have created a whole mythology around it. It tells us, we think, that in the face of adversity, we just need a little British stiff upper lip. It tells us to brace for impact, as if once hit by the boom, it is all predetermined and all we really need is to pick up the pieces and carry on. It is not a good message; we can do more than carry on. And it is a message that wasn't even true at the time.

The poster was never part of any serious war effort. It was produced in 1939 as part of the World War II civilian defense program, but only a few copies were ever seen in public. It wasn't really known about until 2005, when it was uncovered by Stuart Manley, a used bookseller from Northumberland, England, as he was rummaging through old boxes. He put one up on the wall, customers loved it, a few articles were written, and then "all hell broke loose," said Manley, unironically, as it captured the world.

The British War Council never released the poster during the war. It sat in boxes. "Freedom Is in Peril" and "Your Courage, Your Cheerfulness, Your Resolution Will Bring Us Victory" won out. So why was the "Keep Calm and Carry On" message held back throughout the war, even by Churchill? There are a couple of theories, including that Churchill wanted to hold on to it should the British need it for when the country fell to Germany. That's a very different way of looking at the poster. Nobody really knows the exact reason, but my preferred theory is a little simpler: it was a lie. It was too passive. "Keep Calm and Carry On" is not what Churchill needed from the citizens during the literal boom. It was not an honest thing for citizens to hear. Churchill needed Londoners to engage and sacrifice. He needed them to understand that the war was for their lives. It was a fight. He needed the men to go to battle, the women to work in the factories, and children, often alone, to be sent to the countryside. There would be losses,

A motivational poster produced by the British government during World War II.[10]

but fewer losses if the British people took up the fight, took agency, and recognized that they had to deal aggressively with the devil.[11]

To fight an enemy isn't some mental Zen or a mood after impact. It isn't drinking more tea. A war effort isn't calm, and Churchill knew that. Churchill memorably told Parliament in 1940, "We shall fight on the beaches, we shall fight on the landing grounds, we shall fight in the fields and in the streets, we shall fight in the hills; we shall never surrender." Less well remembered is the context for his words: Britain had just experienced a near total catastrophe. Its armies had been plucked at the last moment from the beaches of Dunkirk, sparing them annihilation. The country had surrendered irreplaceable military equipment, which meant it had no short-term prospect of conducting a counterstrike in Europe once it had retreated. And the Blitz was still to come. Churchill had just heard the boom.

THE NOW NORMAL

So here we are. Now. Both before the next and after the last boom, always. It can seem destabilizing. The problems seem so big. Too many of our institutions are careless, negligent, and greedy. True, we can't solve those problems easily. We can, however, continue to learn to lessen their impact. A victory of sorts, until the next time.

At the beginning of the 2020 lockdown, I found myself unable to balance the competing demands of being a professor, a consultant, and a media analyst urging action and response with the demands of, well, me. I suffered from insomnia and a short temper with the kids. I couldn't find my bearings even though I was advising others to do so. I felt that if I could just put my head down and hunker through it that one day, we'd find ourselves on the other side of this hell and in a new normal. I just needed to keep calm and carry on, right?

I am not a religious person. I like to believe that I am spiritual, but it is not really a sophisticated thing. I am more likely to find peace of mind during a long run, in an intense Peloton class, or on a surfboard waiting for the next wave. But I couldn't, for the life of me, find peace during those months. My friend the Reverend Jonathan Walton is the dean of the Divinity School at Wake Forest University. He found himself at the end of many of my despairing questions. How could we survive until the new normal?

Walton gave an online sermon, delivered alone from his iPhone, on the lawn of the North Carolina campus while the world was locked down.[12] His message was clear: don't wait for the new normal, as it will never come. It is a delusion that struggle, disappointment, and deprivation have ever ended. Instead, as he titled his sermon, we must learn to live in the Now Normal. Much of the sermon is about how we can try to ground ourselves in the moment. Perhaps that solace is some religious entity, a poetry book, the recommitment to a marriage or relationship, extra time with children, or, my personal favorite, a Luther Vandross soundtrack. I did a lot of running to Luther that spring and joked with Walton that he had unwittingly founded the Church of Vandross.

But it was Walton's opening to the sermon that drew me in. He, too, has kids and a wife and all the pressures we found ourselves in through that year and beyond. He was surprised where he found the most comfort. It was his late father's words that grounded him, he told the camera. I leaned in close to the screen. What were these wise words from the minister's father? Would they solve everything? Could they, alone, give me ease?

"Life," Walton quotes his father, "just sucks sometimes. It just sucks sometimes."

Yes. The devil never sleeps. But he only wins if we don't do better next time.

You are here.

EPILOGUE

Before the pandemic took over our lives, my last work trip was to CNN's New York City headquarters. I rarely travel to the network. The Boston-based studio worked perfectly fine for when I was needed. But they wanted me to sit with the anchors for coverage of the unfolding pandemic in early March 2020 as its spread was becoming a certainty. Shut it all down, I warned, maybe begged, viewers. Shut it all down.

I drove back to Cambridge the next day. CNN executives were preparing the company's work-from-home announcement, so they told me to leave New York. I did not have a clear concept of how long our isolation would last. Viewers would get used to seeing the backdrops of anchors' and analysts' home offices, bedrooms, and basements. A Twitter feed called Rate My Skype Room became popular as it judged our decorating efforts, highlighting errant wires and bad back lighting.

We had moved around a little in the summer of 2020, and then again in the summer of 2021, for vacation. We drove to the beach and spent some time there. The 2020 holidays were the hardest, though. We used to host an annual Christmas Eve party, an open house for friends and family of all faiths, when more than one hundred people would come in and out during the day. In 2020, it was just the five of us.

I was so wary when I finally went back on the road for work in mid-2021. I had spent the pandemic year busy as all heck, but in sweatpants. I felt as though I had lost my mojo. I joked with a friend that I feared what remained was only "moj." All my systems were off. I didn't even know how to pack. I used to take considerable pride in my packing. Besides the essentials, I could go with one dress per day, two pairs of work shoes, one pair of flats, a blazer, jeans, a top, and running gear. After so long, I couldn't seem to bear leaving any of my stuff behind, even if it didn't fit me quite as well as it once had.

The occasion for my return was as somber as the occasion that had kept me inside for so long. It was the twentieth anniversary of the attacks of September 11, 2001. Twenty years. How did that happen? I was in the counterterrorism field before 2001, and while my jobs had changed, I was never that far from where I started. I was still in the disaster industry. Certainly, I had felt time passing and the day's significance waning over the years through the experiences of my grad students. Most of them were in elementary school when terror struck. They did not feel it like I did. It wasn't a moment in their lives, with those "before/after" and "Where were you when?" elements. They had suffered through endless wars, a financial meltdown, and now the pandemic. They didn't need to adopt our tragedy as well.

CNN had asked me to help with live coverage analysis from New York City. We would televise for five hours under the shadow of the Freedom Tower, the Twin Towers replacement. As I waited to go on early that morning, I met a few members of the New York Police Department gathered close by. They were providing security for the media area. We chatted, as is my habit. Most had been in high school or college on 9/11. At that moment, at that age, they felt moved to join the force. Then, there was very little open discourse about policing in America. The Black Lives Matter movement wouldn't start for over a decade, and our society was in denial of law enforcement misconduct that occurs in so many communities on a daily basis. These were the crises to come. But this anniversary wasn't the time to raise them: 9/11 had changed their lives, luring them to a profession where disasters happen. It was their day too.

The "2021 Special Coverage" was led by Jake Tapper, one of CNN's top hosts. Reporter Garrett Graff, author of the 9/11 book *The Only*

Plane in the Sky, joined as well. We were there to provide analysis and commentary of how the decades had unfolded.[1] I was prepared to play the objective foil to the more heart-wrenching moments from survivors, first responders, and some of the victims' children (who are now all grown up). I was not expecting Tapper's first question. It was simple. "Where were you?"

I can answer that. As I held back the unexpected emotion, I described where 9/11 found me. My daughter Cecilia was just a few weeks old, and I was on maternity leave. I was by chance traveling to NYC with her to visit family that morning on a train heading toward Ground Zero. As news of the tragedy filtered in, the train made a planned stop on its route in Connecticut. Some people got on as if there was something to do in the city. I got off. I told others they should as well. There were no protocols for evacuating a train during a terror attack then. Get off, this counterterrorism expert yelled to the passengers, who did not know much of terrorism an hour before. As I told the story, Tapper asked for more details. I related that it was only then, at that station, that I first saw how the towers fell. From phone calls I had received from reporters looking for experts, I had heard that they had disappeared. There were no iPhones or live feeds then. Pushing my daughter in a stroller toward the station, I finally passed a television set. I saw what it means for the towers to fall. "Where was that?" Tapper continued to press.

"New Haven." I remember everything. "And now she is in college," I said to end the discussion, as if those words neatly summed the twenty years in between.

I was technically accurate. From March 2020 through August 2021, my daughter wasn't actually in school. She finished her first year with us at home, then decided to withdraw from her university. She had a job online; safely, she visited friends in small towns in Kentucky and Colorado to break up the monotony. She was making do with the circumstances, trying to alter the flatness. Once she got vaccinated and her university set rules for return, she reenrolled. I had just dropped her off at college a few days before September 11, 2021.

My daughter lived her nineteenth year with us, but she hoped the following year would welcome a reentry to an adulthood un interrupted by the pandemic. She is out in the world again. It would be unfair to promise her that the devil is gone for good. He will inevitably return, again and again. But on that September 2021 morning, the world seemed less bad. My daughter survived this pandemic in our rambling and cranky house that connected my family to the McCue family and the pandemic before this one.

ACKNOWLEDGMENTS

This book began with two stories. The first described a meeting I had with Jane Cage, a widow from Joplin, Missouri. We remain friends. She was the first to remind me of the devil's return. The second story, about the McCues, was made real by the detectives on Twitter who had me think about my home, and time, differently. I have also learned so much from people who have survived and told their stories of the boom moment. I remain in awe of the first responders and volunteers who run toward danger so they can help others. People often ask me how I remain an optimistic person. The answer is because I see grace and kindness in so many who work in this field. I am grateful to all of them.

Sarah Burnes, my agent, is the most patient and energetic person I have had the privilege of calling a friend. An active participant in fighting for our democracy, she lives and loves much like her great mother. The team at the Gernert Company, especially Sophie Pugh-Sellers, have been invaluable partners.

This has been my first time working with PublicAffairs, and it was such an amazing experience. It was a team effort, and I am grateful to everybody there. Megan Schindele, Michelle Welsh-Horst, Melissa Raymond, and Olivia Loperfido are amazing editorial talents. Lindsay Fradkoff and Jaime Leifer helped guide the book to audiences. Pete Garceau designed the brilliant cover. Anupama Roy-Chaudhury was my partner in so many ways, and I am in awe of her talent at such a young age. Remember her name.

Clive Priddle, my editor, took my Twitter rants about his "British" no-nonsense editorial input with grace. I did not know he was lurking out there, following along. He once called me the one that got away, and that was my mistake. I am glad to have found him. *Tough and inspiring* is a delicate combination, and it is exactly what I needed from him.

I have a career with many pieces, so I hope not to forget anybody. Blame age or COVID; it could be either or both. At the Kennedy School, my "bosses"—Dean Doug Elmendorf, former defense secretary Ash Carter, and Robert and Renee Belfer Center codirector Eric Rosenbach—have always understood how homeland security fits into America's national security efforts. The Belfer family, including Laurence, continue to support my many academic efforts. I am grateful for a faculty grant from the Center for Public Leadership as well and to all my colleagues there and at the Bloomberg Harvard City Leadership Initiative.

Mentors in the homeland security space have led me through my career: Jeh Johnson, Alan Bersin, Ed Davis, Janet Napolitano, Deval Patrick, the late Phil Heymann, Pete Neffenger, Rich Serino, Craig Fugate, Jonathan Wackrow, Courtney Adante, Joe Allen, Bill Bratton, and (the boss of all bosses) Thad Allen. The country is lucky that you all have served and continue to serve her.

So much of this book came out of the opportunity to explore ideas on various media platforms. CNN has been my television home for some time; the brass there, including Jeff Zucker, are great advocates. So many of the CNN hosts and analysts I now consider friends, though we have only met through a box in a studio (or a Cisco link during COVID). Becca Schatz guides me and (often) protects me. Rebecca Kutler first hired me, and I am so excited to see the results of her next project.

The terrific Dante Ramos put me on the pages of the *Atlantic*, where I first started writing about the pandemic and its familiar features in disaster management. His ability to talk through ideas and help focus words proved invaluable. Jeffrey Goldberg is an enthusiastic supporter of this frequent contributor.

The gang at Boston's local NPR station WGBH let me chat away about disasters and national security once a week on the *Boston Public Radio* show. Jim Braude and Margery Eagan are fearless hosts.

Miles O'Brien is a remarkable storyteller, the best in this space (and about space). He and Andy Green, founder and CEO of MyRadar, gave me my first hosting opportunity for a wildly popular digital effort to document how disaster areas recover. The discussion about Paradise, California, came from that project. The pandemic interrupted our travels, but we will return with Suzi Tobias and Michael Linden.

My life as a CEO has taken many turns, so all I can say is that if Andrew Emmons knew how grateful I am to him, he might ask for more equity. Bilal Khan, my cofounder at Grip Mobility, is brilliant and steady. Steve Johnson, whom I met through the most fortuitous encounter, serves to round out this motley crew. Trust the ride, and with you all, I do. Numerous entrepreneurs and investors have let me be a part of their amazing efforts to help protect our nation.

Many thanks to Dominic Gates, Jim Clapper, Daniel Drezner, Nassir Ghaemi, Chris Krebs, Marilyn Darling, and Andy Horowitz for all their time and words. CNN's Jake Tapper and author Garrett Graff were wonderful partners to help end the book. Sadie Golen was a terrific researcher whose enthusiasm was infectious. Christine Heenan, a friend and now neighbor, came up with "you are here" to tie the book together while we were on a dog walk.

And now to the many ladies who call themselves Team Kayyem. How do I thank the amazing young(er) women who support me and my family? I am not worthy of you all, but your dating gossip gives me joy. Tara Tyrell was my faculty assistant for longer than we want to admit; she welcomed my selfies when I made her decide what I should wear. Stacy Hannell has taken over since and has kept the ship running. Dian Lefkowitz and Mallory Heath left the team a while back but have learned the hard way that once you enter, there is really no leaving. Amara Donovan just entered the fold. And Natalia Ariza designed so many of the book's graphics.

And then there is Jamie Sharken. I lied the first day we met and said there wouldn't be more than a few hours of work a week; I told her 2020 was going to be an easy year professionally. Oops. You became my partner and friend, always supportive and smart. You saved me from the "randoms and meanies" who provided too much background noise. You were my best advocate and honest broker.

To the many friends who simply are there for me, I just couldn't be more charmed. The last few years have been hard and isolating, and yet in some ways, they have made our friendships deeper, more necessary. The calls, emails, texts, quick coffees, long walks, DMs, and outdoor drinks gave me life in ways you cannot know. I joke that I am easily pleased. The truth is I am not.

I dedicated this book to my parents for a reason. Simply, thank you. Jon and Marisa, my siblings, are now close friends. You both are funny, brilliant, and supportive, and our family texts give me joy many times a day. Jamie Watts has been so helpful to all the Kayyems, including my parents. I couldn't be luckier with such a large family— all the Kayyems, Watts, Barrons, Weinauers, and Hongs, including the twelve nieces and nephews who fill our lives with so much fun.

My husband, David Barron, does not like a lot of attention. Simply, he has provided more support and love than I deserve while serving this country humbly and with care.

And finally to my children, Cecilia, Leo, and Jeremiah. You remind me every day that being your mother is the greatest privilege and joy in my life. I often sit in wonder and do not know how I got so lucky. I am here, always.

NOTES

PROLOGUE

1. Juliette Kayyem (@juliettekayyem), "A TRUE PANDEMIC MYSTERY SOLVED," Twitter, May 24, 2020, 7:21 a.m., https://twitter.com/juliettekayyem/status/1264532041225441283?s=20.

2. Jane Cage, interview by the author, May 22, 2012.

3. Page 8 Advertisements Column 1, *Cambridge Sentinel*, March 22, 1924, Cambridge Public Library's Historic Cambridge Newspaper Collection, accessed September 23, 2021, https://cambridge.dlconsulting.com/?a=d&d=Sentinel19240322-01.2.38.1&e=-------en-20--1--txt-txIN-------.

4. Miss E. Letitia McCue Obituary, *Cambridge Chronicle*, January 18, 1919, Cambridge Public Library's Historic Cambridge Newspaper Collection, accessed September 23, 2021, https://cambridge.dlconsulting.com/?a=d&d=Chronicle19190118-01.2.83&srpos=1&e=-------en-20--1--txt-txIN-letitia%2Bmccue------.

5. McCue Obituary, *Cambridge Chronicle*, January 18, 1919.

6. Juliette Kayyem (@juliettekayyem), "Now the weird part. Letitia died in January 1919," Twitter, May 24, 2020, 7:21 a.m., https://twitter.com/juliettekayyem/status/1264532055066632192?s=20.

INTRODUCTION

1. Merriam-Webster.com, s.v. "disaster (*noun*)," accessed September 20, 2021, https://www.merriam-webster.com/dictionary/disaster.

2. Scott Gottlieb, *Uncontrolled Spread: Why Covid-19 Crushed Us and How We Can Defeat the Next Pandemic* (New York: Harper, 2021).

3. William W. Prochnau and Laura Parker, *Miracle on the Hudson: The Extraordinary Real-Life Story behind Flight 1549* (New York: Ballantine Books, 2010).

4. Lizzie Johnson, *Paradise: One Town's Struggle to Survive an American Wildfire* (New York: Crown, 2021).

5. "Flooding from Ida Kills Dozens of People in Four States," *New York Times*, September 2, 2021, https://www.nytimes.com/live/2021/09/02 /nyregion/nyc-storm.

6. James McCormick, "International Crises: A Note on Definition," *Western Political Quarterly* 31, no. 3 (September 1978): 352–58, https:// www.jstor.org/stable/447735?origin=crossref.

7. Charles F. Hermann, *International Crises: Insights from Behavioral Research* (New York: Free Press, 1972).

8. Geoffrey A. Rose, *Rose's Strategy of Preventive Medicine: The Complete Original Text* (Oxford: Oxford University Press, 2008).

9. Year 2000 Information and Readiness Disclosure Act, United States: U.S. Government Printing Office, 1998.

10. Francine Uenuma, "20 Years Later, the Y2K Bug Seems Like a Joke. That's Because Those behind the Scenes Then Took It Seriously," *Time*, December 30, 2019, https://time.com/5752129/y2k-bug-history/.

11. Uenuma, "20 Years Later."

12. Robert Meyer and Howard Kunreuther, *The Ostrich Paradox: Why We Underprepare for Disasters* (Philadelphia: Wharton School, 2017).

13. Nassim Taleb and David Chandler, *The Black Swan: The Impact of the Highly Improbable* (Prince Frederick, MD: Recorded Books, 2007).

14. Bryan Appleyard, "Books That Helped to Change the World," *Sunday Times*, March 16, 2010, https://www.thetimes.co.uk/article/books-that -helped-to-change-the-world-qbhxgvg2kwh.

15. Taleb and Chandler, *The Black Swan*.

16. Michele Wucker, *The Gray Rhino: How to Recognize and Act on the Obvious Dangers We Ignore* (New York: St. Martin's, 2016).

17. Arnold M. Howitt and Herman B. Leonard, *Managing Crises Responses to Large-Scale Emergencies* (Washington, DC: CQ Press, 2009).

18. Rebecca Burns, "The Day We Lost Atlanta," *POLITICO Magazine*, January 29, 2014, https://www.politico.com/magazine/story/2014/01/atlanta-snow-storm-102839/.

19. Helen Branswell, "Experts Search for Answers in Limited Information About Mystery Pneumonia Outbreak in China," *STAT*, January 4, 2020, https://www.statnews.com/2020/01/04/mystery-pneumonia-outbreak-china/.

20. Juliette Kayyem, "CNN," JulietteKayyem.com, March 2020, https://juliettekayyem.com/cnn.

21. Juliette Kayyem, "The U.S. Isn't Ready for What's About to Happen," *Atlantic*, March 11, 2020, https://www.theatlantic.com/ideas/archive/2020/03/us-isnt-ready-whats-about-happen/607636/.

22. Ian Bogost, "Now Is the Time to Overreact," *Atlantic*, March 17, 2020, https://www.theatlantic.com/health/archive/2020/03/theres-no-shame-in-overreacting-to-the-coronavirus/608140/.

23. Bogost, "Now Is the Time to Overreact."

24. Bogost, "Now Is the Time to Overreact."

25. Sarah Maslin Nir, "Trapped in Basements and Cars, They Lost Their Lives in Savage Storm," *New York Times*, September 2, 2021, https://www.nytimes.com/2021/09/02/nyregion/nyc-flooding-deaths.html.

CHAPTER 1: ASSUME THE BOOM

1. Graham M. Simons, *Boeing 737: The World's Most Controversial Commercial Jetliner* (Barnsley, UK: Air World, 2021).

2. Rick Townsend, *McDonnell Douglas-Boeing MD-80 Study Guide, 2019 Edition: Covering the MD-82 and MD-83 Versions* (n.p.: Amazon Digital Services LLC—KDP Print US, 2018).

3. Dominic Gates, "FAA Shuts Down Florida Repair Firm That Supplied Faulty Lion Air Sensor on Boeing 737 MAX," *Seattle Times*, October 27, 2019, https://www.seattletimes.com/business/boeing-aerospace/faa-shuts-down-revokes-certificate-of-florida-repair-firm-that-supplied-faulty-lion-air-sensor/.

4. Gates, "FAA Shuts Down Florida Repair Firm."

5. Dominic Gates and Lewis Kamb, "FAA Saw High Risk of Crashes, but Let Boeing 737 MAX Keep Flying," *Seattle Times*, December 12, 2019, https://www.seattletimes.com/business/boeing-aerospace/faa-analysis-after-first-737-max-crash-estimated-high-risk-of-further-accidents/.

6. Bloomberg, "What to Know about the Missing Boeing 737 Jet That Disappeared over Java Sea," *Fortune*, January 10, 2021, https://fortune.com/2021/01/09/boeing-737-plane-crash-indonesia/.

7. Andy Pasztor, "The Airline Safety Revolution," *Wall Street Journal*, April 16, 2021, https://www.wsj.com/articles/the-airline-safety-revolution-11618585543.

8. Bloomberg, "What to Know about the Missing Boeing 737 Jet."

9. Dominic Gates, interview by the author, January 12, 2021.

10. Gates, interview.

11. Cecilia Kang, Drew Harwell, and Brian Fung, "North Korean Web Goes Dark Days After Obama Pledges Response to Sony Hack," *Washington Post*, December 22, 2014, https://www.washingtonpost.com/business/economy/north-korean-web-goes-dark-days-after-obama-pledges-response-to-sony-hack/2014/12/22/b76fa0a0-8a1d-11e4-9e8d-0c687bc18da4_story.html.

12. Jim Clapper, interview by the author, February 5, 2021.

13. Clapper, interview.

14. Fred Kaplan, *Dark Territory: The Secret History of Cyber War* (London: Simon & Schuster, 2016).

15. FEMA, *IS-100.B: Introduction to Incident Command System, ICS-100* (self-pub., CreateSpace, 2017).

16. FEMA, *IS-100.B: Introduction to Incident Command System.*

17. Juliette Kayyem, "Trump Leaves States to Fend for Themselves," *Atlantic*, April 9, 2020, https://www.theatlantic.com/ideas/archive/2020/03/america-has-never-had-50-state-disaster-before/608155/.

18. Andy Slavitt, *Preventable: The Inside Story of How Leadership Failures, Politics, and Selfishness Doomed the U.S. Coronavirus Response* (New York: St. Martin's, 2021).

19. Clapper, interview.

20. Nassir Ghaemi, interview by the author, January 9, 2021.

21. Ghaemi, interview.

22. Alison Escalante, "Why the Zombie Apocalypse Prepared Us for Pandemic Coronavirus," *Forbes*, January 15, 2021, https://www.forbes.com /sites/alisonescalante/2021/01/15/why-the-zombie-apocalypse-prepared -us-for-pandemic-coronavirus/?sh=28623eeb4d46.

CHAPTER 2: WHAT'S THE WORD?

1. Norman MacLean, *Young Men and Fire* (Chicago: University of Chicago Press, 2017).

2. *Canadian Encyclopedia*, s.v. "James Keelaghan," accessed September 27, 2021, https://www.thecanadianencyclopedia.ca/en/article/james-keelaghan.

3. MacLean, *Young Men and Fire.*

4. Stephen J. Pyne, *Smokechasing* (Tucson: University of Arizona Press, 2003).

5. Nicholas Bogel-Burroughs, "F.B.I. Warned of Violence Before Siege; More Arrests Made," *New York Times*, February 18, 2021, https://www .nytimes.com/live/2021/01/12/us/capitol-riot-trump.

6. Tim Hartford, "How to End a Pandemic," *Cautionary Tales*, podcast, July 17, 2020, https://timharford.com/2020/07/cautionary-tales-dark-winter -bright-spring.

7. "Judge Samuel Sewall Survives the 1721 Boston Smallpox Epidemic," New England Historical Society, February 2, 2021, https://www.new englandhistoricalsociety.com/samuel-sewall-survives-boston-smallpox -epidemic-1721.

8. Michael Chertoff, *Homeland Security: Assessing the First Five Years* (Philadelphia: University of Pennsylvania Press, 2011).

9. Jenny Gold and Rachel Bluth, "Is the Bay Area's 'Unprecedented' Lockdown the First of Many?," *Kaiser Health News*, March 17, 2020, https://khn .org/news/is-the-bay-areas-unprecedented-lockdown-the-first-of-many/.

10. Cheryl Guerrero, "Scenes from the 2020 San Francisco Chinese New Year Parade," Hyperlocal Neighborhood News, *Hoodline*, February 10, 2020, https://hoodline.com/2020/02/scenes-from-the-2020-san-francisco -chinese-new-year-parade/.

11. Arthur Conan Doyle, *The Adventure of Silver Blaze: A Sherlock Holmes Adventure* (Paisley, UK: Gleniffer, 1993).

12. Olivier Sibony, Daniel Kahneman, and Cass R. Sunstein, *Noise: A Flaw in Human Judgment* (London: Little, Brown, 2021).

13. Allan J. McDonald and James R. Hansen, *Truth, Lies, and O-Rings: Inside the Space Shuttle Challenger Disaster* (Gainesville: University Press of Florida, 2009).

14. Howard Berkes, "Remembering Allan McDonald: He Refused to Approve Challenger Launch, Exposed Cover-Up," *Morning Edition*, NPR, March 7, 2021, https://www.npr.org/2021/03/07/974534021/remembering -allan-mcdonald-he-refused-to-approve-challenger-launch-exposed -cover.

15. Berkes, "Remembering Allan McDonald."

16. Shankar Vedantam, Rhaina Cohen, Tara Boyle, and Thomas Lu, "The Cassandra Curse: Why We Heed Some Warnings, and Ignore Others," *Hidden Brain*, podcast, NPR, September 17, 2018, https://www.npr.org /2018/09/17/648781756/the-cassandra-curse-why-we-heed-some-warnings -and-ignore-others.

17. Vedantam et al., "The Cassandra Curse."

18. Vedantam et al., "The Cassandra Curse."

19. *Encyclopædia Britannica*, s.v. "Agamemnon," accessed September 30, 2021, https://www.britannica.com/topic/Agamemnon-Greek-mythology.

20. Vedantam et al., "The Cassandra Curse."

21. Scott Gottlieb, *Uncontrolled Spread: Why Covid-19 Crushed Us and How We Can Defeat the Next Pandemic* (New York: Harper, 2021).

22. Riki Ott, *Not One Drop: A True Story of Promises, Betrayal & Courage in the Wake of the Exxon Valdez Oil Spill* (White River Junction, VT: Chelsea Green, 2008).

CHAPTER 3: UNITY OF EFFORT

1. Dina Temple-Raston, "A 'Worst Nightmare' Cyberattack: The Untold Story of the Solarwinds Hack," *All Things Considered*, NPR, April 16, 2021, https://www.npr.org/2021/04/16/985439655/a-worst-nightmare -cyberattack-the-untold-story-of-the-solarwinds-hack.

2. Temple-Raston, "A 'Worst Nightmare' Cyberattack."

3. Edward Davis Company, "Safety Risk Report," East Oakland Stadium Alliance, July 13, 2021, https://www.eastoaklandstadiumalliance.com/safety_risk_report. I assisted Ed Davis on this safety review.

4. Edward Davis Company, "Safety Risk Report."

5. Chris Krebs, interview by the author, April 23, 2021.

6. Krebs, interview.

7. Robin Ferracone, "Good Governance: Do Boards Need Cyber Security Experts?" *Forbes*, July 9, 2019, https://www.forbes.com/sites/robinferracone/2019/07/09/good-governance-do-boards-need-cyber-security-experts/?sh=7faf9aad1859.

8. Kate Conger, "Uber Says 3,045 Sexual Assaults Were Reported in U.S. Rides Last Year," *New York Times*, December 5, 2019, https://www.nytimes.com/2019/12/05/technology/uber-sexual-assaults-murders-deaths-safety.html. I work with Uber on unrelated issues.

9. Steven Norton, "Super Startup Airbnb Must 'Scale Trust' among Users," *Wall Street Journal*, April 18, 2014, https://www.wsj.com/articles/BL-CIOB-4323.

10. Charles W. Wessner, *International Friction and Cooperation in High-Technology Development and Trade: Papers and Proceedings* (Washington, DC: National Academies Press, 1997).

11. Matthew Daley, "TSA to Hire More Screeners to Deal with Long Lines," *Detroit News*, May 25, 2016, https://www.detroitnews.com/story/news/nation/2016/05/25/airport-security/84898162/.

12. Peter Neffenger, interview by the author, March 17, 2021.

CHAPTER 4: AVOID THE LAST LINE OF DEFENSE TRAP

1. Juliette Kayyem, "The Game Changer," *Boston Globe*, April 24, 2011, http://archive.boston.com/news/politics/articles/2011/04/24/the_game_changer/.

2. Kiley Kroh and Michael Conathan, "The Lasting Impact of Deepwater Horizon," Center for American Progress, April 20, 2012, https://www.americanprogress.org/issues/green/news/2012/04/19/11409/the-lasting-impact-of-deepwater-horizon/.

3. Daniel Jacobs, *BP Blowout: Inside the Gulf Oil Disaster* (Washington, DC: Brookings Institution, 2016).

4. D. H. Stamatis, *Failure Mode and Effect Analysis: FMEA from Theory to Execution* (Milwaukee, WI: ASQ Quality, 2003).

5. ManMohan Sodhi and Navdeep Sodhi, "Six Sigma Pricing," *Harvard Business Review*, August 1, 2014, https://hbr.org/2005/05/six-sigma-pricing.

6. E. S. Quade, *The Systems Approach and Public Policy* (Santa Monica, CA: RAND Corporation, 1969), https://www.rand.org/pubs/papers/P4053.html.

7. Center for Food Safety and Applied Nutrition, "HACCP Principles & Application Guidelines," National Advisory Committee on Microbiological Criteria for Foods, U.S. Food and Drug Administration, August 14, 1991, https://www.fda.gov/food/hazard-analysis-critical-control-point-haccp/haccp-principles-application-guidelines.

8. "Role of the Blowout Preventer (BOP) in Drilling Operations," Keystone Energy Tools, August 17, 2021, https://www.keystoneenergytools.com/the-role-of-the-blowout-preventer-bop-in-drilling-operations.

9. "Blowout Preventer 3-1/16IN, 15K, Blind Shear, S/N P09217, w/Skid," IronPlanet, accessed September 25, 2021, https://www.ironplanet.com/jsp/s/item/1991372?utm_source=rbauction&utm_medium=referral&utm_campaign=syndication&src=mktg.

10. Sarah Yang, "Disaster Expert Cites 'Failure to Learn' for Deepwater Horizon Blowout," Center for Catastrophic Risk Management, University of California Berkeley, July 2, 2015, https://news.berkeley.edu/2013/04/18/deepwater-horizon. JS: Deepwater Horizon Study Group, Rep, *Final Report on the Investigation of the Macondo Well Blowout* (Berkeley: University of California, March 1, 2011), https://www.dco.uscg.mil/Portals/9/OCSNCOE/Casualty-Information/DWH-Macondo/DHSG/DHSG-DWH-Investigation-Report.pdf?ver=I-lV-nwDpczeZsPk6JokoQ%3D%3.

11. National Commission on the BP *Deepwater Horizon* Oil Spill and Offshore Drilling, *Deep Water: The Gulf Oil Disaster and the Future of Offshore Drilling*, January 2011, https://www.govinfo.gov/content/pkg/GPO-OILCOMMISSION/pdf/GPO-OILCOMMISSION.pdf.

12. National Commission on the BP *Deepwater Horizon* Oil Spill and Offshore Drilling, *Deep Water*.

13. David Hilzenrath, "When All Hell Breaks Loose: Years after Deepwater Horizon, Offshore Drilling Hazards Persist," Project on Government Over-

sight, December 18, 2018, https://www.pogo.org/investigation/2018/12/when-all-hell-breaks-loose-years-after-deepwater-horizon-offshore-drilling-hazards-persist/.

14. Hilzenrath, "When All Hell Breaks Loose."

15. National Commission on the BP *Deepwater Horizon* Oil Spill and Offshore Drilling, *Deep Water.*

16. Lizzie Johnson, *Paradise: One Town's Struggle to Survive an American Wildfire* (New York: Crown, 2021).

17. Volker C. Radeloff, David P. Helmers, H. Anu Kramer, Miranda H. Mockrin, Patricia M. Alexandre, Avi Bar-Massada, Van Butsic, et al., "Rapid Growth of the US Wildland-Urban Interface Raises Wildfire Risk," Proceedings of the National Academy of Sciences 115, no. 13 (2018): 3314–3319, https://doi.org/10.1073/pnas.1718850115.

18. MyRadar, "Climate Refugees: Paradise—Rebuild or Retreat?," December 23, 2019, YouTube video, https://www.youtube.com/watch?v=B4_IIWVRUTM&t=446s&ab_channel=MyRadar.

19. MyRadar, "Climate Refugees: Paradise—Rebuild or Retreat?"

20. MyRadar, "Climate Refugees: Paradise—Rebuild or Retreat?"

21. Igor Korovin, *Air Crash Investigations: Drama in Sioux City: The Crash of United Airlines Flight 232* (n.p.: Lulu.com, 2011).

22. Korovin, *Air Crash Investigations.*

23. MyRadar, "Climate Refugees: Paradise—Rebuild or Retreat?"

24. Linda Pilkey-Jarvis, Keith C. Pilkey, and Orrin H. Pilkey, *Retreat from a Rising Sea: Hard Choices in an Age of Climate Change* (New York: Columbia University Press, 2016).

25. Pilkey-Jarvis, Pilkey, and Pilkey, *Retreat from a Rising Sea.*

26. Ben Adler, "Congress Passes Biden Infrastructure Plan, the Largest Climate Change Investment in U.S. History," *Yahoo! News*, November 6, 2021, https://news.yahoo.com/congress-passes-biden-infrastructure-plan-the-largest-climate-change-investment-in-us-history-121605735.html.

CHAPTER 5: STOP THE BLEED

1. Dan De Luce, "In the Iraq War, a Revolution in Battlefield Medicine," Medical Xpress, December 11, 2011, https://medicalxpress.com/news/2011-12-iraq-war-revolution-battlefield-medicine.html.

2. De Luce, "In the Iraq War, a Revolution."

3. Eleanor Smith, "Stop the Bleeding," *Atlantic*, September 18, 2014, https://www.theatlantic.com/magazine/archive/2014/10/stop-the -bleeding/379335/.

4. De Luce, "In the Iraq War, a Revolution."

5. Peter Herena, "The Principle of Fail-Safe," ChEnected, Global Home of Chemical Engineers, September 2, 2016, https://www.aiche.org/chenected /2011/02/principle-fail-safe.

6. Greg Bishop, "Behind the Scenes of the Super Bowl Blackout," *Sports Illustrated*, December 22, 2015, https://www.si.com/nfl/2015/12/22/super -bowl-xlvii-blackout-superdome.

7. Bishop, "Behind the Scenes of the Super Bowl Blackout."

8. Bishop, "Behind the Scenes of the Super Bowl Blackout."

9. Judy Battista, "Cause Found for Blackout in Big Game," *New York Times*, February 8, 2013, https://www.nytimes.com/2013/02/09/sports /football/super-bowl-blackout-caused-by-device-meant-to-prevent-it.html.

10. "Why Do Zombies Bleed and How Is That Possible?" Reddit thread, September 13, 2016, https://www.reddit.com/r/zombies/comments/52isr9 /why_do_zombies_bleed_and_how_is_that_possible/.

11. "Zombie Preparedness," Centers for Disease Control and Prevention, February 23, 2021, https://www.cdc.gov/cpr/zombie/index.htm.

12. Daniel W. Drezner, *Theories of International Politics and Zombies* (Princeton, NJ: Princeton University Press, 2015).

13. Daniel Drezner, interview by the author, February 4, 2021.

14. Drezner, interview.

15. Michael Deibert, *When the Sky Fell: Hurricane Maria and the United States in Puerto Rico* (New York: Apollo, 2019).

16. Paul Farmer, Jonathan Weigel, and Bill Clinton, *To Repair the World: Paul Farmer Speaks to the Next Generation* (Berkeley: University of California Press, 2019). Stupid deaths are different from excess deaths. The latter describe the phenomenon, such as during the pandemic, where it is likely that hospitals and public health numbers undercount the true fatality rate. It isn't at all clear we have an exact number of those who died, so we go by what the CDC measures. But there is sufficient research and analysis to suggest that both the national and international numbers are

undercounted, the consequence of factors related to disclosure, causation, and privacy.

17. David Lochbaum, Edwin Lyman, and Susan Q. Stranahan, *Fukushima: The Story of a Nuclear Disaster* (New York: New Press, 2015).

18. "TEPCO to Pay Damages in Fukushima Suicide Case," *BBC News*, August 26, 2014, https://www.bbc.com/news/world-asia-28933726.

19. "The Official Report of the Fukushima Nuclear Accident Independent Investigation Commission," National Diet of Japan, 2012, https://www.nirs.org/wp-content/uploads/fukushima/SaishyuRecommendation.pdf.

20. Alfred Henry Lewis, *Wolfville Nights* (New York: Frederick A. Stokes, 1902).

21. Lewis, *Wolfville Nights*.

22. Mike Zimmerman, "'9 Meals Away from Disaster.' Financial Advisors on How to Prepare for the Worst," *Barron's*, August 23, 2019, https://www.barrons.com/articles/9-meals-away-from-disaster-financial-advisors-on-how-to-prepare-for-the-worst-51566602945.

CHAPTER 6: THE WAY WE WERE

1. Jon Kamp, Will Parker, and Deborah Acosta, "Engineering Firm Warned of Systemic Issue with Miami-Area Condo Building before Deadly Collapse," *Wall Street Journal*, June 26, 2021, https://www.wsj.com/articles/engineering-firm-warned-of-systemic-issues-with-miami-area-condo-building-before-deadly-collapse-11624720688.

2. Kamp, Parker, and Acosta, "Engineering Firm Warned of Systemic Issue with Miami-Area Condo Building Before Deadly Collapse."

3. Konrad Putzier, Scott Calvert, and Rachael Levy, "Behind the Florida Condo Collapse: Rampant Corner-Cutting," *Wall Street Journal*, August 24, 2021, https://www.wsj.com/articles/behind-the-florida-condo-collapse-rampant-corner-cutting-11629816205.

4. "113. Memorandum from Acting Secretary of State Ball to President Johnson," *Foreign Relations of the United States II Vietnam*, no. 3 (February 13, 1965): 614–616, https://doi.org/https://history.state.gov/historicaldocuments/frus1964-68v02/d113.

5. The 9/11 Commission Report: Final Report of the National Commission on Terrorist Attacks upon the United States: Official Government Edition §, Featured Commission Publications (2004), https://www.govinfo.gov/content/pkg/GPO-911REPORT/pdf/GPO-911REPORT.pdf.

6. Mary Louise Kelly, "Clarke Memo Warned of Al-Qaeda Threat," *Morning Edition*, NPR, February 11, 2005, https://www.npr.org/templates/story/story.php?storyId=4494777.

7. Garrett M. Graff, *The Only Plane in the Sky: An Oral History of 9/11* (New York: Avid Reader, 2019).

8. James Clapper, interview by the author, February 5, 2021.

9. Brian K. Sullivan and Naureen S. Malik, "Texas Power Outage: 5 Million Affected after Winter Storm," *Time*, February 15, 2021, https://time.com/5939633/texas-power-outage-blackouts/.

10. Sami Sparber, "At Least 57 People Died in the Texas Winter Storm, Mostly from Hypothermia," *Texas Tribune*, March 15, 2021, https://www.texastribune.org/2021/03/15/texas-winter-storm-deaths/.

11. Miles O'Brien, interview by the author, April 26, 2021.

12. Juliette Kayyem (@juliettekayyem), "Did interview of an expert about a disaster," Twitter, July 8, 2021, 8:58 p.m., https://twitter.com/juliettekayyem/status/1413316603161292801?s=20.

13. Jaikumar Vijayan, "6 Reasons to Hire a Red Team to Harden Your App Sec," TechBeacon, January 22, 2019, https://techbeacon.com/app-dev-testing/6-reasons-hire-red-team-harden-your-app-sec.

14. Gerald J. S. Wilde, *Target Risk 2: A New Psychology of Safety and Health: What Works? What Doesn't? and Why . . .* (Australia: PDE Publications, 2001).

15. J. E. Shealy, C. F. Ettlinger, and R. J. Johnson, "How Fast Do Winter Sports Participants Travel on Alpine Slopes?," *Journal of ASTM International* 2, no. 7 (July 2005). The average speed for helmet users of 45.8 km/h (28.4 mph) was significantly higher than those not using a helmet at 41.0 km/h (25.4 mph).

16. Wilde, *Target Risk 2: A New Psychology of Safety and Health*.

17. B. Hamilton-Baillie, "Towards Shared Space," *Urban Design International* 13 (September 25, 2008): 130–138.

18. Emma Caroline Barrett and Paul R. Martin, *Extreme: Why Some People Thrive at the Limits* (Oxford: Oxford University Press, 2016).

19. Marilyn Darling, Charles Parry, and Joseph Moore, "Learning in the Thick of It," *Harvard Business Review*, August 1, 2014, https://hbr.org /2005/07/learning-in-the-thick-of-it.

20. Darling, Parry, and Moore, "Learning in the Thick of It."

21. Alan Feuer, "Occupy Sandy: A Movement Moves to Relief," *New York Times*, November 10, 2012, https://www.nytimes.com/2012/11/11/nyregion /where-fema-fell-short-occupy-sandy-was-there.html.

22. Richard Serino, interview by the author, April 12, 2019.

CHAPTER 7: THE NEAR MISS FALLACY

1. Dylan Tweney, "Apple's Response to iPhone 4 Antenna Problem: You're Holding It Wrong," *Wired*, June 25, 2010, https://www.wired.com /2010/06/iphone-4-holding-it-wrong/.

2. Avery Hartmans, "'Antennagate' Just Turned 10. Here's How the iPhone 4's Antenna Issues Became One of Apple's Biggest Scandals of All Time," *Business Insider*, July 18, 2020, https://www.businessinsider.com /apple-antennagate-scandal-timeline-10-year-anniversary-2020-7.

3. Diane Vaughan, *The Challenger Launch Decision: Risky Technology, Culture, and Deviance at NASA*, enlarged ed. (Chicago: University of Chicago Press, 2016).

4. Vaughan, *The Challenger Launch Decision*.

5. Vaughan, *The Challenger Launch Decision*.

6. Vaughan, *The Challenger Launch Decision*.

7. Vaughan, *The Challenger Launch Decision*.

8. Vaughan, *The Challenger Launch Decision*.

9. Susan Berfield, "Inside Chipotle's Contamination Crisis," Bloomberg, December 22, 2015, https://www.bloomberg.com/features/2015-chipotle-food -safety-crisis.

10. Berfield, "Inside Chipotle's Contamination Crisis."

11. "Market Capitalization of Chipotle Mexican Grill (CMG)," Companies Market Capitalization, accessed September 29, 2021, https://companies marketcap.com/chipotle-mexican-grill/marketcap/.

12. Peter S. Goodman and Stanley Reed, "With Suez Canal Blocked, Shippers Begin End Run Around a Trade Artery," *New York Times*, March

26, 2021, https://www.nytimes.com/2021/03/26/business/suez-canal-blocked
-ship.html.

13. Chas Danner, "One Big Ship Crisis Ends, It Might Not Be the Last:
Updates," Intelligencer, *New York Magazine*, March 30, 2021, https://
nymag.com/intelligencer/2021/03/ship-still-stuck-leaving-suez-canal
-blocked-updates.html.

14. Lucas Reilly, "The Time 14 Cargo Ships Were Trapped in the Suez
Canal . . . for Eight Years," Mental Floss, September 17, 2018, https://www
.mentalfloss.com/article/557027/time-14-cargo-ships-were-trapped-suez
-canal-eight-years.

15. "When to Skip the Suez Canal for the Cape of Good Hope," Sofar
Ocean, accessed September 29, 2021, https://www.sofarocean.com/posts
/when-to-skip-the-suez-canal-for-the-cape-of-good-hope.

16. Edward Davis, interview by the author, March 19, 2021.

17. Davis, interview.

18. Davis, interview.

19. Catherine Tinsley, Robin Dillon, and Peter Madsen, "How to Avoid
Catastrophe," *Harvard Business Review*, July 16, 2015, https://hbr.org
/2011/04/how-to-avoid-catastrophe.

20. Hans Kuipers, Alan Iny, and Alison Sander, "Building Your Uncertainty Advantage," Boston Consulting Group Global, July 29, 2020, https://
www.bcg.com/publications/2020/using-uncertainty-to-your-advantage.

21. Jen Wieczner, "The Case of the Missing Toilet Paper: How the Coronavirus Exposed U.S. Supply Chain Flaws," *Fortune*, May 21, 2020, https://
fortune.com/2020/05/18/toilet-paper-sales-surge-shortage-coronavirus
-pandemic-supply-chain-cpg-panic-buying/.

22. Wieczner, "The Case of the Missing Toilet Paper."

23. Wieczner, "The Case of the Missing Toilet Paper."

CHAPTER 8: LISTEN TO THE DEAD

1. *Smithsonian Magazine*, "These Century-Old Stone 'Tsunami Stones'
Dot Japan's Coastline," Smithsonian.com, August 31, 2015, https://www
.smithsonianmag.com/smart-news/century-old-warnings-against-tsunamis
-dot-japans-coastline-180956448/.

2. Eric Orts and Joanne Spigonardo, *Disasters, Leadership and Rebuilding—Tough Lessons from Japan and the U.S.*, Initiative for Global Environmental Leadership, October 2013, http://d1c25a6gwz7q5e.cloudfront.net /reports/2013-10-01-Disasters-Leadership-Rebuilding.pdf.

3. Law and Public Policy Asia-Pacific, "Lessons in Leadership from the Fukushima Nuclear Disaster," Knowledge@Wharton, University of Pennsylvania, October 3, 2013, https://knowledge.wharton.upenn.edu/article /lessons-leadership-fukushima-nuclear-disaster/.

4. "The Official Report of the Fukushima Nuclear Accident Independent Investigation Commission," National Diet of Japan, 2012, https:// www.nirs.org/wp-content/uploads/fukushima/SaishyuRecommendation .pdf.

5. Greg Allen, "A New Hurricane Season Brings a New Threat: Carbon Monoxide Poisoning," *Morning Edition*, NPR, June 1, 2021, https://www .npr.org/2021/06/01/1000203891/a-new-hurricane-season-brings-a-new -threat-carbon-monoxide-poisoning.

6. Alan R. Earls and Michael S. Dukakis, *Greater Boston's Blizzard of 1978* (Chicago: Arcadia, 2008).

7. Dave Cullen, *Columbine* (New York: Grand Central, 2009).

8. John A. Kolman, ed., *Patrol Response to Contemporary Problems: Enhancing Performance of First Responders through Knowledge and Experience* (Springfield, IL: Charles C. Thomas, 2006).

9. Peter Nickeas and Elyssa Cherney, "Critics Warn School Shooter Drills May Be Doing More Harm Than Good: 'They're Becoming More Perverse and Obscene,'" *Chicago Tribune*, February 12, 2020, https://www .chicagotribune.com/news/ct-active-shooter-drills-schools-lockdowns -20200212-dzfevmvj6zfyla6eyj52d42uq4-story.html.

10. Ethan Siegel, "Science Busts the Biggest Myth Ever about Why Bridges Collapse," *Forbes*, May 24, 2017, https://www.forbes.com/sites/starts withabang/2017/05/24/science-busts-the-biggest-myth-ever-about -why-bridges-collapse/?sh=94a2f3f1f4c0.

11. Nickeas and Cherney, "Critics Warn School Shooter Drills May Be Doing More Harm Than Good."

12. Michael Babaro, "Facebook vs. the White House," *Daily*, podcast, *New York Times*, July 20, 2021, https://www.nytimes.com/2021/07/20

/podcasts/the-daily/facebook-misinformation-biden-vaccine-skeptics
.html.

13. Sheera Frenkel and Cecilia Kang, *An Ugly Truth: Inside Facebook's Battle for Domination* (London: Bridge Street, 2021).

14. "The Facebook Files," *Wall Street Journal*, September 15, 2021, https://www.wsj.com/articles/the-facebook-files-11631713039.

15. Andy Horowitz, *Katrina: A History, 1915–2015* (Cambridge, MA; London: Harvard University Press, 2020).

16. Andy Horowitz, interview by the author, April 28, 2021.

17. Horowitz, *Katrina*.

18. Dick Gilbreath, *The Indian Ocean Tsunami: The Global Response to a Natural Disaster* (Lexington: University Press of Kentucky, 2011).

19. Matthew Lauer, "Oral Traditions or Situated Practices? Understanding How Indigenous Communities Respond to Environmental Disasters," *Human Organization* 71, no. 2 (2012): 176–187, http://www.jstor.org/stable/4414864.

20. Monica Lindberg Falk, *Post-Tsunami Recovery in Thailand: Sociocultural Responses* (Abingdon, UK: Routledge, 2015).

21. "Tsunami, 10 Years On: The Sea Nomads Who Survived the Devastation," *Guardian*, December 10, 2014, https://www.theguardian.com/global-development/2014/dec/10/indian-ocean-tsunami-moken-sea-nomads-thailand.

CONCLUSION

1. Associated Press, "Don't Get Too Shaken Up, but Richter Scale Is Defunct," *Deseret News*, April 28, 1994, https://www.deseret.com/1994/4/28/19105909/don-t-get-too-shaken-up-but-richter-scale-is-defunct.

2. Art Bell and Whitley Strieber, *The Coming Global Superstorm* (New York: Pocket Books, 2004).

3. Florko, "New Chart Reveals Military's Vast Involvement."

4. Judith Rodin, *The Resilience Dividend: Being Strong in a World Where Things Go Wrong* (New York: PublicAffairs, 2014).

5. Rodin, *The Resilience Dividend*.

6. "Climate Change Widespread, Rapid, and Intensifying," Intergovernmental Panel on Climate Change, United Nations, August 9, 2021, https://www.ipcc.ch/2021/08/09/ar6-wg1-20210809-pr/.

7. Seth Borenstein, "'Code RED': UN Scientists Warn of Worsening Global Warming," AP NEWS, Associated Press, August 10, 2021, https://apnews.com/article/asia-pacific-latin-america-middle-east-africa-europe-1d89d5183583718ad4ad311fa2ee7d83.

8. Greg Ip, "IPCC Climate Change Report Shows Less Cause for Panic—But More Urgency to Act," *Wall Street Journal*, August 12, 2021, https://www.wsj.com/articles/ipcc-climate-change-report-gives-a-less-extreme-but-more-sobering-outlook-11628697997.

9. Ryan Mulcahy, "Climate Scientist on UN Report: Just as Bad as We Expected," *Harvard Gazette*, August 13, 2021, https://news.harvard.edu/gazette/story/2021/08/climate-scientist-on-un-report-just-as-bad-as-we-expected/.

10. "Keep Calm and Carry On," poster, World War era, accessed October 1, 2021, https://worldwarera.com/products/keep-calm-carry-on-poster.

11. Bex Lewis, *Keep Calm and Carry On: The Truth Behind the Poster* (London: Imperial War Museums, 2017).

12. Wake Forest University, "The Now Normal," March 29, 2020, YouTube video, https://www.youtube.com/watch?v=5rQoit9BxAA&ab_channel=WakeForestUniversity.

EPILOGUE

1. Garrett M. Graff, *The Only Plane in the Sky: An Oral History of 9/11* (Waterville, ME: Thorndike, 2020).

INDEX

Index

In academia, the private sector, government, and media, Professor Juliette Kayyem is an international leader in crisis management, disaster response and homeland security. Kayyem is presently on the faculty at Harvard's Kennedy School of Government. Previously, she served as President Obama's assistant secretary at the Department of Homeland Security. A CNN national security analyst, Pulitzer Prize finalist, and frequent contributor to the *Atlantic*, Kayyem also advises governors, mayors, and corporations on crisis management. She is the author or editor of six books, including *Security Mom*. Kayyem has three children and lives in Cambridge, Massachusetts, with her husband.

PublicAffairs is a publishing house founded in 1997. It is a tribute to the standards, values, and flair of three persons who have served as mentors to countless reporters, writers, editors, and book people of all kinds, including me.

I. F. STONE, proprietor of *I. F. Stone's Weekly*, combined a commitment to the First Amendment with entrepreneurial zeal and reporting skill and became one of the great independent journalists in American history. At the age of eighty, Izzy published *The Trial of Socrates*, which was a national bestseller. He wrote the book after he taught himself ancient Greek.

BENJAMIN C. BRADLEE was for nearly thirty years the charismatic editorial leader of *The Washington Post*. It was Ben who gave the *Post* the range and courage to pursue such historic issues as Watergate. He supported his reporters with a tenacity that made them fearless and it is no accident that so many became authors of influential, best-selling books.

ROBERT L. BERNSTEIN, the chief executive of Random House for more than a quarter century, guided one of the nation's premier publishing houses. Bob was personally responsible for many books of political dissent and argument that challenged tyranny around the globe. He is also the founder and longtime chair of Human Rights Watch, one of the most respected human rights organizations in the world.

.   .   .

For fifty years, the banner of Public Affairs Press was carried by its owner Morris B. Schnapper, who published Gandhi, Nasser, Toynbee, Truman, and about 1,500 other authors. In 1983, Schnapper was described by *The Washington Post* as "a redoubtable gadfly." His legacy will endure in the books to come.

Peter Osnos, *Founder*